Research Teaching and Learning

in

Higher Education

EDITED BY

**BRENDA SMITH
AND SALLY BROWN**

**KOGAN
PAGE**

Published in association with the
Staff and Educational Development Association

D0280418

The Staff and Educational Development series
Series Editor: Sally Brown

Assessing Competence in Higher Education Edited by Anne Edwards and
Peter Knight

Assessment for Learning in Higher Education Edited by Peter Knight

Research, Teaching and Learning in Higher Education Edited by Brenda Smith
and Sally Brown

Kogan Page Limited
120 Pentonville Road
London N1 9JN

British Library Cataloguing in Publication Data

A CIP record for this book is available from the British Library.

ISBN 0 7494 1412 X

Typeset by DP Photosetting, Aylesbury, Bucks
Printed and bound in Great Britain by
Biddles Ltd, Guildford and King's Lynn.

Contents

Notes on Contributors

Dorothy Bell is Information Assistant in MARCET, the Materials and Resources Centre for Enterprising Teachers, in the Educational Development Service of the University of Northumbria at Newcastle.

David Boud is Professor of Adult Education at the University of Technology, Sydney, Australia.

Angela Brew is Director of the Educational Development Unit at the Academic Development Centre of the University of Portsmouth.

Reva Berman Brown is Co-director of the MBA programme in the Department of Accounting and Financial Management at the University of Essex.

Sally Brown is an Educational Development Adviser in the Educational Development Service of the University of Northumbria at Newcastle.

Marshall Elliott is Director of Research in the Business School of the University of Sunderland.

Lewis Elton is Professor Emeritus of Higher Education at the University of Surrey and Higher Education adviser to the Department of Employment.

Della Fazey is a Lecturer in the School of Education at the University of Wales, Bangor and the Project Director for the two-year Guidance and Learner Autonomy Project, funded by the Department of Employment.

John Fazey is a Senior Lecturer at the University of Wales, Bangor and is Director of the Staff Development Unit there.

David Garnett is the Director of Teaching and Learning in the Faculty of the Built Environment at the University of the West of England at Bristol.

Graham Gibbs is the Head of the Oxford Centre for Staff Development and Professor at Oxford Brookes University.

Michael Gregory is the Head of the Faculty of Business and Management at Suffolk College.

Roy Gregory is Principal Lecturer in Engineering Education in the Mechanical and Aero Engineering Division of the University of Hertfordshire.

Irene Harris is Business Development Manager in the Faculty of Management and Business of Manchester Metropolitan University.

Roy Holmes is Professor of Facilities Management at the Faculty of the Built Environment at the University of the West of England at Bristol.

Terri Kelly is the interim Director of the Centre for Continuing Education, Development and Training at the University of Hull.

Sean McCartney is Co-director of the MBA programme in the Department of Accounting and Financial Management at the University of Essex.

Liz McDowell is an Educational Development Adviser in the Educational Development Service of the University of Northumbria at Newcastle.

Ian Moore is a Staff and Educational Developer at the University of Ulster.

Mike O'Neil is Principal Lecturer in Higher Education at the Nottingham Trent University.

Phil Race is Professor of Educational Development at the University of Glamorgan.

Brenda Smith is Teaching and Learning Quality Manager at the Nottingham Trent University.

Peter Smith is Professor of Computing in the Department of Computer and Information Systems at the University of Sunderland.

Lin Thorley is Head of Learning Development at the University of Hertfordshire.

Frank Walkden is Head of the Learning System Institute of the University of Salford.

Tom Wengraf directs the Higher Education Action Research and Design Unit at Middlesex University.

Foreword

This book is based on sessions and keynote speeches at the SEDA (Staff and Educational Development Association) Conference on Research Teaching and Learning held at Dyffrwn House, Cardiff in November 1993. SEDA conferences are active and participative, so these chapters are not for the most part papers that were read at the confence; rather they represent the reworked and distilled thoughts of the presenters after they had had the experience of leading a workshop on a related topic.

Leading a participative conference session is not the same kind of activity as writing or reading aloud a learned paper. The designation 'workshop' recognizes, as does good teaching practice in universities today, that effective learning in higher education is not a matter of passive reception of ideas from a single authority, but of sharing, cooperation and interaction between a group of adults, guided by a sensitive facilitator who is able to manage the process of learning as well as contributing from his or her own personal experience, knowledge and expertise.

Thanks are due to the organizing committee for the conference, led by Joyce Barlow and Richard Kemp. We are grateful to all those who have contributed to this publication, either by writing chapters or by helping us in its production, particularly Trisha Little of the University of Northumbria at Newcastle; we also recognize the leadership and support the organization SEDA gives to all those who are committed to ensuring the effectiveness of those working in higher education in all facets of their academic practice.

Sally Brown

SECTION ONE

THEORETICAL PERSPECTIVES

Chapter 1

Research, Teaching and Learning: Issues and Challenges

Brenda Smith and Sally Brown

INTRODUCTION

This book is timely, originating as it does from a lively and well-attended conference exploring the relationships between research, teaching and learning in the academic environment. It is in two halves, the first seven chapters exploring some theoretical perspectives on the key issues and chapters 8 to 18 demonstrating how some of these ideas work in practice in universities.

In this first chapter, we take the opportunity to review some of the fundamental questions affecting the research and teaching functions of British universities in the 1990s, in times which in terms of the Chinese curse are 'interesting'. In so doing, we aim to introduce some of the key themes and also to argue our particular view that research and teaching should be equally valued as complementary and essentially mutually supportive activities at the heart of the work of academics in higher education.

In Chapter 2 Graham Gibbs writes about what we can learn about student learning, using significant existing research that, although available, is all too often unrecognized or ignored. Angela Brew and David Boud write next about the need to develop an understanding of the relationship between research and teaching in order to maximize the potential for both. This is followed by a chapter in which Lewis Elton explores the effects the policies of the Funding Councils have on teaching quality.

Next David Garnett and Roy Holmes look at what they see as the symbiotic relationship between research, teaching and learning, demonstrating really fruitful interaction between undergraduate and postgraduate teaching and learning. In Chapter 6, Peter Smith and Marshall Elliott discuss the current and future importance of applied as opposed to basic and strategic research, which has resulted in a much more applied and practical orientation to many research projects.

In the final chapter of this section Frank Walkden writes about ways of improving learning by training individuals to be proactive in their approaches to study, rather than relying overmuch on sequential models of teaching.

Section Two commences with Phil Race's lively gallop through the tensions between academic research and student-centred learning, teasing out the broad competences which underpin both good quality teaching and research.

The next three chapters are concerned with research students and their supervision: Chapter 9 by Lin Thorley and Roy Gregory addresses the development and problems of a research methodology course for research students and looks at some of the mechanisms in use to help them to cope with researchers who also teach while completing their research theses. Ivan Moore next describes how they are trying to provide staff development for the supervisors of such students at the University of Ulster and in Chapter 11 Irene Harris explains how the Business and Management faculty at Manchester Metropolitan University has set up and run a programme for research-related staff development.

The next group of chapters describe initiatives to research the effectiveness of teaching and learning: the first of these outlines a SEDA-funded small scale research project by Dorothy Bell, Sally Brown and Liz McDowell using repertory grid techniques to explore lecturers' perceptions of what makes a good lecturer. This is followed by Mike O'Neil's chapter which includes essential principles for enhancing high quality learning in higher education and suggestions on how to foster a learning environment in which deep learning can take place.

Next Michael Gregory writes about the background and design of an MA in Human Resource Management where action learning and action research provide the model for accrediting professional development. In Chapter 15, Della and John Fazey report some key outcomes of their work on a sport, health and physical education programme in which commitment to teaching stems from the need to apply knowledge about learning to the course itself, putting into practice the principles they prescribe.

In Chapter 16 Sean McCartney and Reva Berman Brown review the use of research learning on self-identified projects on a part-time MBA at Essex University, where students become more effective learners by adopting a deep approach, thereby enabling the tutors to become facilitators rather than content deliverers. Tom Wengraf next describes how 49 of his first-year students were asked to interview a sample of students and tutors on how best to improve a specific module on a course and then to produce a report to a strict format: the results are fascinating!

Finally Terri Kelly discusses the often troubled relationship between staff and educational development and provides an idiosyncratic view of the way this is progressing in her own institution. We conclude with a brief Afterword in which we make some proposals on the way forward in the coming years: a manifesto for research, teaching and learning in higher education.

WHY DO OUR UNIVERSITIES WANT US TO CONCENTRATE MORE ON RESEARCH?

The Research Selectivity exercise puts urgent pressure on universities to encourage lecturers to become active researchers in order to secure associated funding. The system is still in a state of flux, but the race for a starred 5 looks set to be a pressure on all traditional universities. At the same time, institutions which in the first exercise were quite happy to have achieved a 2, given the comparatively minimal research funding previously available to them under the old system, now feel the pressure to do much better, if they are to maintain the funding they have got.

The system is so susceptible to all kinds of political pressures that it seems certain that some universities will make grave errors of judgement in the decisions they make in how they direct their efforts. Lewis Elton's chapter on the effect of Funding Council policies on teaching quality is most illuminating in this respect. Current thinking seems to suggest that institutions which have traditionally been badly funded for research and which have insubstantial backgrounds in research would be foolhardy to invest too much time or money in improving their research ratings at the expense of their teaching quality. It seems certain that the changing system is still likely to privilege the former high flyers at the expense of those lower down the scale. We must not, however, give up the fight to be effective in research too.

CONFLICTING PRESSURES: RESEARCH AND TEACHING QUALITY

Perfectly competent university lecturers who see teaching as their principal function are now being made to feel unproductive and undervalued if they do not have a string of publications to their names. This is being felt particularly badly in the former public sector institutions, which have traditionally had a stronger bias towards teaching, whereas lecturers in the old universities have always been required to be active in research and publishing. Lecturers from the new universities, however, are nowadays expected to be as active in research as they are in teaching, although rarely is compensatory time allowed to enable meaningful research activities to be undertaken.

Simultaneously, lecturers from the older universities are being exhorted to concentrate more on the techniques of effective teaching, a pressure that is not always welcome. A letter from a lecturer in a large civic university in the North East, quoted in Evans (1993), illustrates such a view:

> I am not a teacher. I am not employed as a teacher, and I do not wish to be a teacher. I am employed as a lecturer, and in my naivety I thought that my job was to 'know' my field, contribute to it by research, and to lecture on my specialism. Students may attend my lectures but the onus to learn is on them. It is not my job to teach them.

Apocryphal stories are common of advice given by old hands to newly recruited lecturers in old universities to have as little to do with the students as possible, to leave lectures promptly without allowing time for questions and to maintain a closed office or lab door so as to preserve from contamination the precious time available for research. In this way they will be able to achieve academic success and career advancement. The new universities are not immune from such thinking: a respected senior research chemist known to the editors was heard to advise a group of new lecturers on a postgraduate teaching certificate course that if they worked hard and achieved success in research, they might, like him, be able to get out of teaching completely.

To academics for whom involvement with students has often been seen as a tangential rather than a central task, the movement towards student-centred learning is a radical one and just as disruptive to their view of what they are supposed to be doing as is the experience of teachers in the old public sector now being cajoled or coerced into active research.

How can we balance our research and teaching activities?

This is perhaps the hardest question to deal with. Many university lecturers are finding that they are under pressure to teach more and more students with no more resources, just at a time when they are expected to produce graduates with a range of skills and abilities attractive to employers: simultaneously lecturers are urged to adopt new, creative and student-centred teaching approaches. To be expected to undertake meaningful research as well is proving to be the last straw for many.

In some disciplines and departments it is relatively easy to ensure that the research one is undertaking is so closely linked to the subjects one is teaching that the two activities support each other. Elsewhere, hard-pressed academics are trying to keep up with their research interests, while their teaching areas are becoming more and more divergent. For many, the research they are doing is often unrelated to their teaching load, and instead of enhancing and reinforcing it, research work actually ends up as a competitive demand on their limited time. We frequently hear of lecturers, especially in the new universities, who are given teaching timetables at the last minute which require detailed preparation, often *ab initio*, with no assurance that they will be teaching the same material again in the following year, or indeed, ever again.

Most universities have an element of research and scholarly activity as a specified requirement within a lecturer's workload: in some cases, this can lead to lecturers seeking out areas to research which have minimal long-term value in their contribution to scholarship, but which are undertaken because they are manageable and achievable. This kind of drudgery benefits no one.

Publications which are produced as a result of a need to fulfil an annual quota of research output will tend not to be ground-breaking or exciting. In science, technology and engineering research, it is now considered better to split a set of research findings into ten short papers published in a selection of journals, rather than to compile an excellent and substantial single contribution to the discipline ('salami slicing'). Just as people had got used to the idea that it was important to produce as many publications as possible, the rules changed again and now the watchword is quality not quantity, with active researchers being asked to put forward for consideration their four best publications within a set period rather than all of their publications. It is no wonder that academics feel themselves stretched to the limits.

One of the problems of those who are trying to break into publication is that many journals act as a closed shop, only publishing papers by what the police call KTUs (Known To Us), whether this is an overt process or what Belbin terms 'elective homogeneity' (Belbin, 1981) by which groups tend to perpetuate themselves by recruiting to their own image. Reputedly, one of the unfairnesses of the first research selectivity exercise was the way in which publications only counted if they were in designated 'reputable journals', and this list of journals has been established by the panels, based on their own preconceptions and opinions, rather than any more balanced view (Cross, 1994). This view can be crudely paraphrased as 'If we haven't heard of this journal and we don't know any of the names on the editorial panel it can't be much good'.

Journals are springing up around the country which have been devised purely to provide refereed and therefore countable publication outlets for researchers (within the grounds of profitability, of course). Those involved in editing any kind of academic publication can testify to the massively increased submission rate of materials for publication and also the increased number of slightly desperate phone calls one receives enquiring whether items have been accepted, so that people can include them in their research ratings.

In the former polytechnics, people who have quietly been ticking away, publishing sometimes quite arcane texts, often regarded by their colleagues as perhaps slightly self-indulgent and certainly rather odd, suddenly find themselves sought after and celebrated. There are rumours of a lucrative transfer market for academics with good publications track records, and people who haven't seriously addressed themselves to writing since the early days of their academic careers are suddenly feeling the hot breath of the departmental head of research on the backs of their necks!

The authors even know of a small, active, original but rather off-beat social science research group which has split itself into two halves, one half being the editorial panel of the International Journal of XX and the other half acting similarly for the British Journal of XX. Thus members of each half can submit papers to the other half for publication without unnecessary interference from hostile referees!

Not surprisingly, respected journals not only are heavily over-subscribed with potential contributors, but also have long waiting lists of accepted papers. We know of authors being told, 'Yes, we will be delighted to publish this, but it will have to be in an issue towards the end of next year!' The result of such pressure is a new kind of performance indicator for journals, that of speed of publication. After all, researchers could be entitled to think that the most important criterion is that the paper is published in time for the next research selectivity exercise, which is only interested in papers in print, not accepted or at press.

WHAT IS SCHOLARLY ACTIVITY?

As the pressure to be 'active' grows (were we all so inactive before?!), the definition of what comprises research is being reviewed; correspondence in the *Times Higher Education Supplement* (Frayling, 1994), for example, begs the question whether 'arty facts', that is writings about art, are really superior in output terms to artistic artifacts. Should the definition of what research consists of take greater account of the diversity of academic practice in universities? Should not works of art, sculptures, paintings, fashion garments, etc. be permitted to count in the same way that creative writing (novels, poems, plays) often are?

We believe it is time to review the hierarchies: to look again at the relative value of letters in the press, in-house publications (often effectively vanity presses), conference presentations, workshops and keynote speeches. How can we compare the relative merits of writing and editing publications? Can we find ways of breaking down the old boys' networks (sadly there is often a gender dimension) which control access to publication in many disciplines? What constitutes an international publication and are some countries of publication more reputable than others?

Frequently co-authored texts are seen as being inferior to those that have single authors: is this necessarily the case? Naturally we, the co-editors of this book, feel that there are unarguable benefits to cooperation in writing and research. Indeed, we have found that co-authoring with a range of colleagues has been one of the most significant sources of our own professional and personal development. To write collaboratively is a highly developed skill, requiring negotiation, tact, teamwork, sensitivity, all the kinds of abilities that we would hope to promote in our students. And yet we are warned to be cautious about over-reliance in our publications records on joint work, which is often deemed to be rather dubious. ('How can we know how much she was *really* responsible for?')

Of course there are also games that can be played with joint publication: we all have heard of the researchers who tactically co-publish even when collaboration has been minimal in order to bulk up their individual paper counts. We also know of more sinister activities when research supervisors claim credit for the work of their research students by insisting on their names going first in the author order of co-written texts, even when their actual contribution to the writing has been nil.

We would argue that the rules that govern what does and does not count as scholarly activity in universities need to be dismantled, redesigned and rebuilt, so that the system does not unfairly privilege the conventional over the innovative. Those of us who currently work in the old public sector keenly feel a sense of injustice, that we are not competing for research funding on an even footing with the old universities. If we are all to be able to compete on equal terms for research funding (and there is some question about whether this will continue for long to be the case), then the proverbial playing field must be a level one, and the goal posts, once fairly fixed in place in properly regulated positions, must stay still, at least until the system is established and understood by all parties.

RESEARCH ABOUT TEACHING AND LEARNING

If we are to improve the quality of teaching and learning in our universities, we need to find out about the relative merits of the different techniques available to us. Graham Gibbs' chapter reminds us that most of the major questions many of us would like to see answered about teaching and learning in higher education have already been addressed in the past 20 years, particularly in the USA.

In Britain in the last ten years there has been considerable research into what works and what does not in university teaching, but it is only recently that the disciplines of staff and educational development have become a recognized and respectable area. Only comparatively recently have we seen the appointment of professors of educational development at one end of the scale and of research students looking into issues of pedagogy (and androgogy) in higher education at the other. However, the field is growing, as the success of SEDA, the Staff and Educational Development Association, can testify. At one stage the establishment of staff and educational development units was largely to be found in former polytechnics, but now, due in part to the pressures of the HEFC quality assessment exercise, which directs attention to the quality of teaching in all universities, these are becoming more commonly found in old universities too.

Only by applying rigorous and relevant research techniques to teaching techniques will we ever be able to convince doubters of the efficacy of the methods many of us believe in with passionate conviction. Such research is currently piecemeal: we need to organize and participate in much more systematic approaches to research about teaching and to be much more effective at disseminating such research as already exists.

REFERENCES

Cross, M (1994) Unpublished lecture material from a presentation given at the University of Northumbria at Newcastle, 28 January.

Belbin, RM, (1981) *Management Teams: Why they succeed or fail*, London: Heinemann.

Evans, C (1993) *English People: the experience of teaching and learning English in British Universities*, Buckingham: Open University Press.

Frayling, C (1994) 'Artifacts or arty facts' Opinion Column, *Times Higher Education Supplement* May 20.

Chapter 2

Research into Student Learning

Graham Gibbs

At a CVCP/SRHE research seminar on teaching and learning, Noel Entwistle said: 'much of the work on innovations in teaching and learning has a rather weak research base' (Entwistle, 1993). In the same week the National Commission on Education reported and recommended that more research into effective teaching and learning practices should be undertaken and that some kind of national unit be set up to undertake and coordinate this research. We need to ask ourselves whether more research is really necessary and if so, of what kind and undertaken by whom.

We already know a good deal. The evidence shown in Table 2.1 comes from a very large-scale piece of educational research. What might Condition C be that it results in such a dramatic improvement in student performance?

In fact the 'experiment' involved the whole of higher education in the UK over 21 years and the three 'conditions' are the years 1969, 1979 and 1990 (MacFarlane, 1992). The point about this evidence is that few believe that standards have actually improved and it raises far more questions than it answers. It would be helpful to have some evidence about some of these questions. For example haven't the larger classes which have mushroomed since 1979 led to poorer performance, not better performance? Well actually they have, and we have clear evidence about this. For example in a study of the relationship between module enrolment and student grade on 1,500 modules involving 37,000 students over five years, students in large classes were found to have a significantly lower chance of getting good grades (see Table 2.2).

Table 2.1 *Student performance under three conditions*

| | Condition | | |
	A	B	C
Proportion of students gaining 1sts or 2:1s	29%	32%	49%

This is extremely clear evidence and if it had been taken seriously it would have led to a reconsideration of the strategies being adopted for coping with increased student numbers. Unfortunately the institution involved ignored the evidence (as did the rest of higher education) and more than trebled the number of modules with enrolments of over 70 over the next five years. And we now have preliminary evidence that the relationship between class size and performance is stronger than it was ten years ago.

We also have good research evidence about the effects of class size at a micro-level: on student and teacher behaviour in seminars, for example. We know that the proportion of teacher talk increases with class size and that as class size increases, students talk less and their questions and answers get shorter and the cognitive level of their contributions declines so that in groups of 16 and over the majority of student contributions are at the lowest (knowledge) level (Mahler *et al.*, 1986). This has not stopped seminar sizes increasing to 16 and beyond in most institutions.

At the same research seminar where Entwistle claimed that innovation had a poor research base, Alistair MacFarlane (author of the MacFarlane Report, 1993) said that it was inevitable that students would have to pay their own fees. We have clear evidence that this, too, would be highly damaging. A study in one institution found that even without having to pay fees students accumulated debt at a rate of £1,350 a year if they didn't work. As a result, 93 per cent of students undertook part-time paid work at some time during their studies. Failure on a module was found to be three times higher for students who undertook part-time work during that module and on average students undertaking part-time work gained significantly lower marks. This led to an estimated 250 students a year getting a lower class of degree than they would have otherwise have and 1,640 modules a year being retaken to replace failures due to part-time work (Paton-Saltzberg and Lindsay, 1993).

What Noel Entwistle didn't say is that even when we have the evidence we ignore it. And despite the effects of large classes on performance, the effects of large seminars on the quality of student involvement and the effects of part-time work on student failure, more students than ever before are gaining good degrees. Now that really is worth researching.

Table 2.2   *Module enrolment and student grades 1981–5*
(Lindsay and Paton-Saltzberg, 1987)

Module enrolment	% of students gaining grades of A or B+
1–20	40%
>70	28%

Clear quantitative evidence just doesn't seem to carry the weight that it should and academics can be extraordinarily irrational about evidence once outside their own discipline area, especially educational evidence. For example, what conclusion might one reasonably draw from the summary of 23 research studies comparing teaching method X with a range of alternatives, shown in Table 2.3? In these studies educational benefit was measured by students' ability to analyse cases, solve problems, synthesize evidence and so on.

Method X is, of course, lecturing – the most common teaching method in higher education. This evidence has been available for over 20 years but has had little impact on the prevalence of lecturing. When confronted with evidence of this kind, lecturers' most common reaction is to find some objection, either concerning methodology or differences in context, which are argued to reduce the relevance of the findings to zero. If someone doesn't want to believe that lecturing is a relatively poor teaching method then no amount of evidence will make any difference.

In this context calls for more research seem to miss the point. There is a huge body of research evidence out there but it is either not known about or ignored. It is hard to imagine what further research on lecturing, for example, could make any difference to the business of changing compulsive lecturers' minds. Quantitative studies which compare method A with method B provide imaginative academics with endless fun thinking up alternative explanations and additional questions which need researching before any clear conclusion can be drawn. When I hear someone ask me for 'hard evidence' to back up my suggestions about practice, I can predict the course the interaction will take, because the only kind of evidence which this kind of person claims would convince them also offers them unlimited opportunities for evasion.

An alternative approach to using individual pieces of quantitative research evidence is to undertake large-scale reviews and only present the broad conclusions which can be drawn from these reviews. An excellent example is the 'Seven principles for good practice in undergraduate education' published by the Ford Foundation (Chickering and Gamson, 1987):

Table 2.3 *Summary of 23 research studies comparing method X with alternatives (from Bligh, 1972)*

Method X Worse	No Difference	Method X Better
18 studies	5 studies	0 studies

1.   Good practice encourages student-faculty contact

2.   Good practice encourages cooperation among students

3.   Good practice encourages active learning

4.   Good practice gives prompt feedback

5.   Good practice emphasizes time on task

6.   Good practice communicates high expectations

7.   Good practice respects diverse talents and ways of learning.

This kind of list has face validity and is backed up by extensive literature and comprehensive analysis. In the USA these principles have had a major impact and institutions are taking them seriously in reviewing and improving courses. A conference is devoted to reporting action implementing these principles and already a book has been written containing examples of implementing these principles (Chickering and Gamson, 1991).

Also in the USA the Department of Education funds (to the tune of $6 million) a unit at Penn State University (The National Center on Post Secondary Teaching, Learning and Assessment) to collate research findings and disseminate them in accessible forms. Their job is not to undertake research – there is already plenty of that – but to make sense of it and communicate it in appropriate ways. They do this in short summaries and in 'The Teaching Professor' – an A4 news sheet with 20,000 subscribers.

In her workshop at the conference, Liz Beaty described powerful ideas lecturers ought to know about, that at conferences on student learning in the late 1970s a small group of researchers used to talk to each other, and to no one else, and had no impact on practice. I was one of those researchers and very depressing it all was! In contrast, at Warwick University in September 1993, 170 people came to a research symposium on Improving Student Learning and over 75 per cent of them were lecturers. Most of the papers were by lecturers who were using research frameworks and research tools to make sense of their own teaching and their own courses. This represents a sea change in attitudes and behaviour, which is, in this country at least, in part due to the CNAA-funded Improving Student Learning project in which lecturers were supported by funds and expertise to study changes in their courses designed to increase the extent to which students took a deep approach in their learning. Reported in leaflets to 30,000 people and through two conferences, a book (Gibbs, 1992) and more than 30 workshops, it made use of a well-articulated framework based on existing research and applied it as best it could. The remainder of this chapter summarizes that framework and the research findings and research tools associated with it, and gives a range of brief examples of the ways in which it has been applied to improve student learning as reported at the Improving Student Learning symposium.

The research framework, based originally on work in the 1970s by Marton in Sweden and Biggs in Australia, has four main elements. First, students go about learning in qualitatively different ways. The approach students take to their studies can be seen to involve either an intention to make sense (a deep approach) or an attempt to reproduce (a surface approach). Second, the *outcomes* of student learning are not just quantitatively different, they are also qualitatively different – students understand different kinds of things, structured in different ways, not just more or less. Third, students understand what learning itself is, what knowledge is, and what they are doing when learning, in profoundly different ways, seeming to develop over time in the sophistication of their conception of learning. Fourth, teachers understand what teaching and learning consist of, and therefore what 'good teaching' should consist of, in profoundly different ways.

The most important research tools associated with this framework are first, categories of description of approach, conception of learning and conception of teaching, allowing interview data to be categorized reliably and meaningfully. Second, the SOLO (structures of observed learning outcomes: see Biggs and Colliss, 1982) taxonomy enables the easy categorization of the structural qualities of learning outcomes. Third, questionnaires (there are several, but I will refer to the ASI or Approaches to Studying Inventory) allow easy measurement of the extent to which students generally take a surface or deep approach. Fourth, questionnaires (the best and most recent being the Course Experience Questionnaire [CEQ]) allow easy measurement of students' perceptions of key features of courses which are known to influence students' approach.

The following extremely brief summary of the main research findings from within this framework provided the context for the studies which I will then go on to report.

- Students vary in their approach from context to context. Most students take a deep or surface approach depending on the context. A few students always take a surface approach. Most courses have students taking both approaches to some extent. A surface approach is very prevalent.

- A surface approach nearly always leads to poorer quality learning outcomes: little understanding and only short-term recall of information. It also leads to poor marks and degrees when the assessment system rewards the outcomes of a deep approach. A deep approach can lead to good understanding, good long-term recall and better marks and degrees.

- Students develop in their conceptions of learning and in their conceptions of knowledge.

- Students' conceptions of good teaching are closely related to their conception of learning – those who have crude conceptions of learning believe teaching should be teacher-centred.

- Study skills can be used to implement either a surface or a deep approach. Crude conceptions of learning constrain the approach chosen. So the appropriate focus of learning-to-learn courses is on conceptions of learning, knowledge and tasks, not on techniques.

- Students tend to take a surface approach when the workload is perceived to be heavy and where the assessment system is perceived to demand, reward or tolerate memorization and in a number of other known circumstances.

- Students tend to take a deep approach where they are motivated to understand, where they are active, where they discuss what is to be understood, and where they encounter knowledge in well-structured ways.

- It is possible to change students' approach and the quality of their learning outcomes by manipulating those features of the context which the research has identified as crucial and especially by changing the assessment system.

Very crudely, the research can be summarised in three statements:

'Quantitative conceptions of learning don't get students very far'

'Quantitative conceptions of teaching don't get teachers very far'

'Quantitative conceptions of research don't get educational researchers very far'.

Much research and evaluation assumes that characteristics of teaching, such as the methods used, have a direct impact on learning outcomes, as in Figure 2.1, or that student characteristics, such as their educational background or study skills, have a direct impact, as in Figure 2.2.

The model underlying current research into student learning is more complex and assumes that the most important features involve percep-

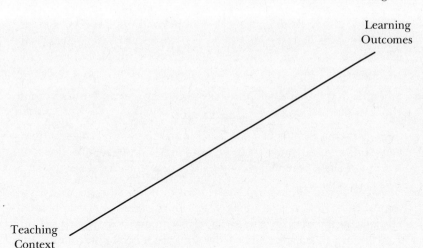

Figure 2.1 *A teaching-centred model of learning*

tions, by teacher and students, of the context. While approach is the most important factor relating to learning outcomes, there are several precursors which influence approach, as in Figure 2.3. Another feature of this more complex model is that the influences operate in both directions. For example, if a student realizes that factual outcomes from taking a surface approach are in fact sufficient to get adequate marks, this will change their perceptions of the course and the approach they will then adopt will be affected.

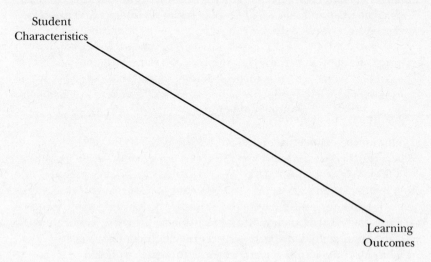

Figure 2.2 *A student-centred model of learning*

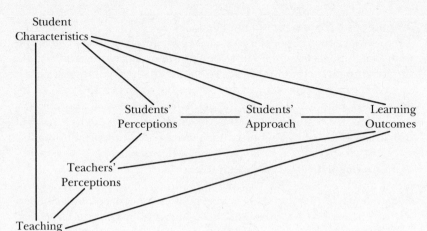

Figure 2.3   *An interactive model of learning*

This research framework and these research tools were used in a wide variety of ways in the papers reported at the Warwick Improving Student Learning symposium. Six types of use are listed here and one example given of each.

1 Monitoring entire degree programmes
Gregory *et al.* (1993) studied 20 degree and other courses (involving nearly 1,000 students) in a large engineering school using the Course Experience Questionnaire (CEQ). They identified several degrees with low scores on most of the crucial scales (such as good teaching, appropriate workload, appropriate assessment). This has led to workshops with appropriate staff and study of student workload and assessment tasks in the courses concerned in order to identify more clearly what is causing the problems. The CEQ enabled them to identify and diagnose problems in a way which conventional evaluation would not.

2 Monitoring changes in modules
Blackmore and Harries-Jenkins (1993) reported a study, involving the use of the ASI, of several very large business and accountancy modules into which open learning materials had been introduced and teaching greatly reduced. In one module, student performance had markedly declined. The ASI showed that student motivation had progressively declined, a surface approach had progressively increased and a deep approach had progressively declined. The conceptual framework helped to diagnose the causes of the problems and this had led to a range of specific changes.

3 Monitoring changes within modules

Tang (1993) studied the introduction of longer assignments alongside traditional short-answer tests in a context where short-answer tests and a surface approach were common. It was found that students took a surface approach to preparation for the short tests but a deeper approach to the longer assignments. However, inexperienced students inappropriately retained a surface approach to the longer assignments, highlighting the need to introduce new methods with an eye to how students will respond.

4 Diagnosing individual student problems

Meyer and Parsons (1993) used the ASI and other devices to identify at-risk students early on in their studies and enable early intervention to reduce the likelihood of failure. In contrast Leitch (1993) reported several attempts to identify at-risk students using an atheoretical statistical method (discriminant analysis) which had not been successful. The clear implication is that you need a theoretical framework and that purely statistical approaches are unlikely to be successful.

5 Designing curricula and assessment criteria

Jackson (1993) described the structure and operation of a degree programme in graphic information design designed around fundamental principles from student learning research, including conceptions of learning and the SOLO taxonomy, to define goals and levels of achievement which translate into project briefs and assessment criteria.

6 Rewarding excellence in teaching

Lublin and Prosser (1993) recast their institution's evaluation and promotion mechanisms around a definition of good teaching derived from student learning research:

> Good teaching is teaching which helps students to learn. It discourages the superficial approach to learning and encourages active engagement with the subject matter ... it encourages in the learner motivation to learn, desire to understand, perseverance, independence, a respect for the truth and a desire to pursue learning.

The important difference between these studies and the quantitative evidence cited at the start of this chapter is that the authors were, by and large, not trying to persuade others but were exploring their own teaching using a framework which they understand and which made sense to them. They were using research and research tools to intervene, often successfully, in their own courses. This is the kind of research which gets results. This brings me to the concluding points I wish to make about research into student learning, which are about who should be doing what kinds of research.

Professional researchers should concentrate on fundamental research developing theory, principles and research tools, *with the aim of empowering teachers.*

Teachers should be doing research on their own courses and teaching, using these theories and tools. I am not talking here about theory-free action research which tends to hold out the promise of eventually rediscovering the wheel, or student feedback collection which, without a theoretical underpinning, provides little basis for understanding what is going on.

A national body, with a specialist research team, should be set up and charged with *making existing research accessible to teachers and policy makers.* They should not be undertaking research themselves, but should be collating existing findings. Their main focus should be on communicative effectiveness.

Finally, *educational developers should be undertaking four main roles*:

- *Supporting teachers' research.* This might involve research training, acting as a 'free' researcher on their behalf, and helping with interpretation and writing.

- *Disseminating* the output of the national unit's collations of research findings.

- *Undertaking institution-wide research*, beyond the confines of individual courses. In universities in the USA or Australia, this role may be performed by a special institutional research outfit. In the absence of such outfits in the UK it falls on educational developers to keep their senior management informed of the key changes taking place within the institution in order to inform policy.

- *Using research to direct institutional policy* on issues such as course review, evaluation and promotion. Some institutions are imposing comprehensive student feedback systems which are not capable of performing the quality enhancement function they were designed for. Educational developers should be sufficiently well-informed to be able to explain the inappropriateness of such measures.

REFERENCES

Biggs, JB and Colliss, KF (1982) *Evaluating the Quality of Learning: the SOLO taxonomy*, New York: Academic Press.

Blackmore, MA and Harries-Jenkins, E (1993) 'Open learning: the route to improved learning?', Improving Student Learning Symposium, Warwick.

Bligh, DA (1972) *What's the Use of Lectures?*, Harmondsworth: Penguin.

Chickering, AW and Gamson, ZF (1987) 'Seven principles for good practice in undergraduate education' (special insert) *The Wingspread Journal*, 9, 2.

Chickering, AW and Gamson, Z (1991) *Applying the Seven Principles for Good Practice in Undergraduate Education. New Directions for Teaching and Learning. No.47*, San Francisco, CA: Jossey Bass.

Entwistle, N (1993) 'Teaching and the quality of learning. What can research and development offer to policy and practice in higher education?', CVCP/SRHE Research Seminar, London.

Gibbs, G (1992) *Improving the quality of student learning*, Bristol: Technical and Educational Services.

Gregory, R, Thorley, L and Harland, G (1993) 'Using a standard student experience questionnaire with engineering students – initial results', Improving Student Learning Symposium, Warwick.

Jackson, B (1993) 'Course design for learning: towards improving student learning in new courses', Improving Student Learning Symposium, Warwick.

Leitch, A (1993) 'Improving study skills: an experimental approach', Improving Student Learning Symposium, Warwick.

Lindsay R and Paton-Saltzberg, R (1987) 'Resource changes and academic performance at an English polytechnic', *Studies in Higher Education*, 12, 2.

Lublin, J and Prosser, M (1993) 'Implications of recent research on student learning for institutional practices of evaluation of teaching', Improving Student Learning Symposium, Warwick.

MacFarlane, A (1993) *Teaching and Learning in an Expanded Higher Education Section* (The MacFarlane Report), HEFCE.

MacFarlane, B (1992) 'The Thatcherite generation and university degree results', *Journal of Further and Higher Education*, 16, 2.

Mahler, S, Neumann, L, Gurion, B and Tamir, P (1986) 'The class-size effect upon activity and cognitive dimensions of lessons in higher education', *Assessment and Evaluation in Higher Education*, 11, 1.

Meyer, JHF and Parsons, PG (1993) 'Conceptually at risk students: diagnostic and intervention strategies based on individual differences', Improving Student Learning Symposium, Warwick.

Paton-Saltzberg, R and Lindsay, R (1993) 'Do students get too much work?', *Teaching News*, 35, Autumn.

Tang, C (1993) 'Effects of modes of assessment on students' preparation strategies', Improving Student Learning Symposium, Warwick.

Chapter 3

Research and Learning in Higher Education

Angela Brew and David Boud

A great deal of research has been undertaken on the relationship between research and teaching in higher education. In looking at this research, we came to the conclusion that it appeared to have reached an impasse and was no longer contributing usefully to the debates about the role of teaching and research in higher education. We thought that it might be more productive to consider the relationship between learning and research rather than teaching and research as a starting point. In the workshop on which this chapter is based, we wanted to present our thoughts on work which had been done principally in the USA and Australia on the relationship between teaching and research and then to explore with participants the links between learning and research.

The workshop was established as an investigation. We had developed a number of ideas about what we considered to be the links between learning and research (Brew and Boud, submitted for publication) and we hoped that participants would assist us in exploring these further. If, from their collective experience, they identified similar linkages, the ideas we had could be validated. If, on the other hand, they came up with something rather different, this would mean we had some rethinking to do.

In the workshop, participants first shared the issues that interested them and in groups raised questions that they wished the workshop to address. Then the literature on teaching and research was introduced. This was by way of setting a context for the discussions which were to follow. Participants then divided into groups according to whether they identified with the role of researcher or the role of learner/facilitator of learners. Two groups were asked to consider, as researchers, what they learn from doing research and how. They were asked to be specific and to put their ideas on green 'post-it' notes. Two groups were asked to consider, as facilitators of learners, in what ways/ how they can use research to help people to learn. Again they were asked to be specific but to put their ideas on yellow post-it notes. The four groups then stuck the notes on a flipchart and the similarities and differences were compared. After further discussion in the large group about the superficial nature of what is meant by research and teaching in the literature, 'yellow' and 'green' groups came together in two larger groups to consider the hypothesis that the vital link between research and teaching is learning, using all the post-its and questions to inform their discussions.

As expected, the 22 participants brought a broad range of questions to the workshop. Some of these had been addressed in the literature on research and teaching (such as whether it is possible to correlate good teaching and good researching); others were addressed more directly in the workshop discussions ('How does research affect learning – as opposed to teaching?' and, 'How do you get students to see their learning as "research"?') or featured in our initial questions ('Are there examples of research following teaching/learning initiatives?', 'What input should research have into different courses at different levels?'). Some questions drew the concept of scholarship into the debate ('Are universities still about scholarship?', 'How should scholarship be defined?').

In this chapter, the context of research into the links between research and teaching is first established. This is followed by a discussion of our initial conceptions and how they were modified and elaborated in the small group discussions. Finally some general conclusions about conceptualizing the relationships between research and learning are drawn.

THE LINK BETWEEN TEACHING AND RESEARCH: MYTH OR REALITY?

There is a very widely held view among teachers and researchers that there is a relationship between research and teaching in higher education. Ramsden and Moses (1992) present three views of the links: the strong integrationist view which suggests that in order to be a good university teacher you have to be an active researcher; the integrationist view which is the belief that there are links between teaching and research at the departmental or institutional level but not at the level of the individual academic. The third view is an unpopular one: this they call the independence view and, as the name suggests, it asserts that there is no causal relation existing between the two.

It is clear from the research which has been done that the belief that there is a link is stronger than the link. In one study carried out in the USA (Centra, 1983) 95 per cent of science faculty staff agreed that 'research increases teaching effectiveness by increasing awareness and currency', but they also said that a good teacher did not have to do research. The research on senior academics by Neumann (1992) in Australia, shows that perceptions of the relationship between teaching and research are complex and subtle. Neumann draws attention to the differences between people's perceptions and their actual practice. In her study she found consensus in beliefs and values about the link between teaching and research, but recognized that her subjects may have been representing what they believed the ideal beliefs and values to be, as opposed to what they actually did. There is clearly a disjuncture between the widely held view amongst academics that there is a link and the results of many empirical studies.

Research on the links between teaching and research, of which there is a great deal, has failed to establish the nature of the connection between them nor, indeed, whether there is one. In spite of numerous studies which have been done, the nature of the relationship eludes us. In his review of numerous studies in the USA, Feldman (1987) concluded that although the relationships were almost always positive, more often than not they were statistically insignificant. He found that the small correlation which exists when research is measured by publication counts, indicators of research support and peer ratings, disappears when research is measured by citation counts: the measure which appears to come closest to measuring the quality of research productivity. How often your work is cited is, it seems, unrelated to your teaching effectiveness.

A change in the way teaching or research is measured, then, will affect the correlation. In another US review, Webster (1985) looked at nine studies all of which concluded that there is little or no positive correlation between research productivity and teaching effectiveness. Ramsden and Moses (1992) go further. In their study of associations between research and undergraduate teaching among Australian academics they found negative or near-zero correlations both at the individual and the departmental level.

Measures of teaching and research are not easily come by. Many studies have combined data from a number of places, or used data collected for other purposes. But in using existing data too many assumptions have had to be made, for example, about how the data were gathered as well as about what precisely was measured. When we say that a small correlation exists, questions arise as to its scope; for example whether it applies at an individual level or whether it relates to a collective correlation. If a link is found at the individual level, does this mean it is true over an entire career span or is it, as Centra (1983) suggests, related to a person's age, or the stage of their career or to general ability and energy levels?

There are further problems if what is being compared are disciplines and institutions. Some researchers have found correlations between teaching and research in the natural sciences (Frey, 1978; Hoyt and Spangler, 1976), while another (Centra, 1983) failed to find correlations in these disciplines but found them in social sciences. The problem is that scales which use numbers of publications are discipline-specific, a point which the Higher Education Funding Councils would do well to note in relation to research selectivity. As different disciplines clearly give different results (Centra, 1983), there are problems of translating findings across disciplines. There are in any case problems of inferring causal linkages from correlations. So, if you want to establish a link over all disciplines and in all kinds of institution, the problems are immense.

The way in which the research findings are interpreted is dependent on the interpreter's underlying beliefs about the link. Indeed, the weakness of the association which is found in many studies appears to be unrelated to the conclusions which are drawn. The widely-held view that there is a link means that researchers continue to do studies rather than drawing the obvious conclusion that no link exists. The fact that further studies are undertaken suggests an unwillingness to accept that there is very little correlation. Indeed, researchers have repeatedly questioned why there are low or no correlations. The implicit assumption appears to be that there 'is really' a link, or that there 'ought to be' a link, but that we have simply failed to demonstrate it statistically. The results which we do have are not so much conflicting as inconclusive. Webster (1985) says the myth that there is a link between teaching and research persists because we would like there to be a link. This means that there is no way anyone could show that the assumed link does not exist.

The research findings are consistent with the idea that it is not teaching and research that are directly (if weakly) related, but that each is related to something else:

> it is essential to search out and consider the possible availing and countervailing forces that may be at work as well as to sort out causal from noncausal relationships. In this way factors that may mediate the causal effects of research productivity on teaching effectiveness can be distinguished from 'extraneous' factors that may merely produce the appearance of a causal relationship between research productivity and teacher effectiveness by affecting each one separately. (Feldman, 1987, p. 247)

We would suggest that such a link is learning. We have come to the conclusion that the debate about the links between teaching and research has become sterile. We suggest that a much more productive question is: what is the nature of the relationship between learning and research?

THE WORKSHOP INQUIRY

At the start of the inquiry, participants were unaware of the ideas which we had previously formulated. They were asked to divide themselves according to whether they identified with the role of researcher – 'Researchers' – or the role of learner/facilitator of learners – 'Learners'. The 'Researchers' were given the task of identifying what they learned from doing research and how; the 'Learners' were asked to identify ways in which they can use the methods of research to help people to learn. In this section, we look at our initial ideas and the ways in which they found expression or otherwise in the groups' findings.

We had noted the way in which studies on the relationship between teaching and research focused on knowledge as the acquisition or discovery of something existing externally from the people who were either generating or discovering it on the one hand, or transmitting or handing it over on the other. We ourselves have been concerned to view knowledge as a construction. Learning and research are both, for us, about creating knowledge. They both refer to the way people come to know. That means making sense of fuzzy reality; discovering meaning in hitherto seemingly unconnected phenomena and pre-existing ideas. This is to suppose a chaotic experiential process. But of course learning always takes place in a cultural context so it is also constrained. Research similarly has this character of being chaotic, in terms of the individual researchers' sense-making but constrained by socially acceptable methodologies. These issues were alluded to by the 'Researchers'. They referred to dealing with complexity and uncertainty yet doing so within constraints. The process, they suggested, dominates results. In this context, Feyerabend's observations are pertinent:

> A scientist starts with a bulk of material consisting of diverse and conflicting ingredients. There are theories formulated in accordance with the highest standards of rigour and precision side by side with unfounded and sloppy approximations, there are solid facts, local laws based on some of these facts, there are heuristic principles, tentative formulations of new points of view which partly agree, partly conflict with the accepted facts, there are vague philosophical ideas, standards of rationality and procedures that conflict with these. Being unable to make such material conform to simple views of order and consistency the scientist usually develops a practical logic that permits him to get results amidst chaos and incoherence. (Feyerabend, 1978, p.199)

The 'Learners' recognized that the processes of research are similar to those that students go through and suggested that in teaching you are therefore a learner helping other learners. Research can therefore inform practice in facilitating learning. There was the recognition that Kolb's (1984) experiential learning cycle can map both processes. And the question was asked whether research, scholarship and learning were different names for Kolb's learning cycle.

The question: 'In what ways/how can you use research to help people to learn?' elicited several thoughts about the role of chaos and ambiguity. There was the idea that research undermines certainties and promotes tolerance of ambiguity/uncertainty and also that research and learning both involve questioning one's own knowledge and understanding. The question, 'What do you learn from doing research?' led the 'Researchers' to identify a number of 'skills' eg, learning how to put down information in a precise form, ability to turn 'hunch' into theory, asking the right questions, methodologies, skills such as word processing, data processing and data analysis. Doing research is, they suggested, multidisciplining. Interestingly, all of these skills would be useful to students whatever their area of study.

We recognized that research and learning are more often than not directed towards different ends. Research leads to public outcomes, for example, books, journals and reports. Yet not all of the outcomes of research enter the public domain. Most of the individual learning which researchers do in the course of their research remains private. This includes what they learn about themselves and the skills they develop, as well as findings which do not fit the overall pattern of explanation but which may inform future research. Workshop participants looking at what you learn during research suggested they learnt personal attributes and development. They learnt to recognize their ignorance and to identify the limits of their personal skills and the need for team support. They also recognized the value of debate with peers. Learning may also remain a private activity. However, workshop participants looking from the learners' perspective drew attention to the issue of opening what is learnt to public scrutiny, for example through questioning by peers and the idea of joint explorations by teachers and learners.Learning is often an individual activity whereas research is more commonly characterized by teamwork. There is, however, overlap and this statement is clearly subject-specific. Teamwork is less common, for example, in the humanities than it is in the sciences. Workshop participants who were looking from the learning perspective viewed project work by groups and individuals and independent study as close to research and suggested they help in developing analytical skills and synthesis and the habit of rigour. But also importantly, they contribute to independence rather than dependence among learners. These suggestions indicate that workshop participants agreed with our assessment that research is akin to the adoption of a deep approach to learning where learners take responsibility for their learning rather than a surface approach in which students directly respond to their perceptions of their teachers' demands.

In the literature described earlier, we find a rather surprising absence of any discussion of what research is and what teaching is. In order to conduct the studies, good teaching and research are defined by the way they are measured. But this gives a rather instrumental view of teaching and research. For example, research has been measured by: number of publications (Linsky and Straus, 1975), citation score, faculty membership in a university research society, judgements of departmental heads (Hoyt and Spangler, 1976), and research grants received (Bresler, 1968).

Examining the measures of good teaching one finds there too a somewhat mechanistic notion of teaching. There is, generally, an absence of explicit discussion of the kind of teaching being referred to but an implicit assumption that teaching is the imparting of subject-specific knowledge, and that the task of the teacher is to hand over that knowledge to the student. The measures referred to in the literature discussed above must be seen in that context. A knowledge-centred teaching and learning system (Murgatroyd, 1980) is presupposed. A package view of knowledge is presented in which there is a separation between knower and what is known, and an emphasis on quantitative, detached, impersonal knowledge. If we look at learning in the way workshop participants did, we see a more interactive view.

To measure research by publications or even by citation counts, is to focus on the outputs of the research rather than the process of doing it. It makes the assumption that research is principally about the creation of a body of knowledge which is detached or separated off from the people who developed it. It is what Popper (1972) called 'knowledge without a knower'. It is knowledge which denies the value of the human subjective processes which have gone into establishing it; the doubts and difficulties of researchers as they grapple with hard ideas and complex problems and it denies too the learning and growing which researchers have done in order to produce the 'measurable' outputs, ie, publications (Feyerabend, 1975).

If we bring learning in as the link and see research as a process of learning we see that:

Research is a process of learning. Indeed research is the process whereby much learning proceeds. This is as true of the three year old discovering the garden for the first time as for the analytical chemist or the quantum physicist in their sophisticated laboratories. Research is learning. This is almost a truism; it's obvious. (Brew, 1988, p.1)

This is perhaps a bold assertion. But in our workshop we saw what happens when you ask a group of teachers, learners and researchers to make the links between research and learning. Those looking from the researchers' perspective suggested that research is about 'identifying key ideas (creativity), identifying similarities (cross-fertilizing) and the excitement of discovery (learning).' The discussion appears to have led to our conclusion expressed by those looking from the learners' perspective, that: 'research and learning are not separable.'

CONCLUSION

Politically the stakes are loaded against evidence showing there is not a link between teaching and research. Neither staff, who wish to be allowed to continue to engage in both teaching and research, nor institutional managers who want to maintain university funding based upon research and teaching have any desire to see the link severed or weakened. In spite of talk about raising the profile of teaching, research still has higher status in higher education. Debates about the division of institutions into research institutes and teaching-only universities; about the reward and recognition for teaching excellence; about the use and exploitation of staff who are labelled teachers as opposed to researchers; about whether, following the research selectivity exercise institutions should concentrate on teaching or on research – all rest on the belief that there is a link between teaching and research; a belief which, as we have seen, is not substantiated by the inconclusive research.

Because of these beliefs and the political consequences which follow, there is an inherent but generally unrecognized bias in the design of studies and in the interpretation of findings. It is interesting to note that the assumption is that research productivity enhances teaching effectiveness and not the other way round. There are few arguments that being good at teaching makes for better research. Yet this might equally be inferred from the small correlations that exist. It is part of the political justification that research makes you better at teaching. These political issues are acknowledged by Ramsden and Moses (1992) who argue that research performance should not act as a surrogate for teaching performance, that separation of teaching and research may increase teaching quality and that students should not be misled into thinking highly selective, highly productive research departments offer high quality courses.

One way of considering the research findings has been proposed by Elton, who was one of the 'Researchers'. He suggests (1986) that scholarship is the link between teaching and research. It is, he suggests, different from both teaching and research. Scholarship in both discipline and pedagogy is concerned with new and critical interpretations of what is already known (Elton, 1992). Elton thus makes a distinction between the reinterpretation of existing knowledge and the discovery of new knowledge and suggests that this is not just a philosophical argument. It affects funding decisions, for example. Elton's concern is for the application of scholarship and the consequent reflective practice both to the subject discipline and to teaching. He recognized that engaging in scholarship is engaging in a learning process.

The 'Learners' asked the question of whether 'inquiry' was a more helpful term and the word 'study' was also suggested. One group of 'Researchers' clearly had difficulty initially in thinking of research as a learning process. The concept of scholarship may have assisted this. It is unhelpful here, however, to get into a debate about the meanings of words. We would suggest though that what characterizes research, teaching, scholarship, inquiry and study is learning. Whether we emphasize research or inquiry; teaching or learning; scholarship or study has to do with the relationship of the individual to the context and content of that learning. It also has to do with the underlying assumptions about the nature of knowledge which are made. We choose to focus on the idea of knowledge as a construction. It is an individual construction and it is a social construction. Whether knowledge is new depends on the individual engaging with it. But it also depends on the social context wherein it was conceived.

We do not deny that there is a link between teaching and research. We wish to point out though that it is neither very helpful nor very meaningful to talk about it in this way. Nor do we deny that scholarship is an important concept in the discussions, particularly those about funding. In this chapter we have outlined what happened when we offered the opportunity for a group of academics to explore the links between learning and research. It was an exploration. However, the findings suggest that it is a fruitful focus for work in this area.

REFERENCES

Bresler, J B (1968) 'Teaching effectiveness and government awards', *Science*, 160, 164–7.
Brew, A (1988) 'Research as learning', PhD thesis, University of Bath.
Brew, A and Boud, D (submitted for publication) 'Teaching and research: establishing the vital link with learning'.
Centra, J A (1983) 'Research productivity and teaching effectiveness', *Research in Higher Education*, 18, 4, 379–89.

Elton, L (1986) 'Research and teaching: symbiosis or conflict', *Higher Education*, 15, 299–304.

Elton, L (1992) 'Research, teaching and scholarship in an expanding higher education system', *Higher Education Quarterly*, 46, 3, 252–68.

Feldman, K A (1987) 'Research productivity and scholarly accomplishment of college teachers as related to their instructional effectiveness: a review and exploration', *Research in Higher Education*, 26, 3, 227–98.

Feyerabend, P (1975) *Against Method*, London: Verso.

Feyerabend, P (1978) *Science in a Free Society*, London: Verso.

Frey, P W (1978) 'A two-dimensional analysis of student ratings of instruction', *Research in Higher Education*, 9, 1, 69–91.

Hoyt, D P and Spangler, R K (1976) 'Faculty research involvement and instructional outcomes', *Research in Higher Education*, 2, 1, 81–8.

Kolb, D A (1984) *Experiential Learning*. Englewood Cliffs, NJ: Prentice-Hall.

Linsky A S and Straus, M (1975) 'Student evaluation, research productivity and eminence of college faculty', *Journal of Higher Education*, 46, 1, 89–102.

Murgatroyd, S (1980) 'What actually happens in tutorials?', *Teaching at a Distance*, 18, 44–53.

Neumann, R (1992) 'Perceptions of the teaching-research nexus: a framework for analysis', *Higher Education*, 23, 2, 159–71.

Popper, K (1972) *Objective Knowledge: An evolutionary approach*, Oxford: Oxford University Press.

Ramsden, P and Moses, I (1992) 'Associations between research and teaching in Australian higher education', *Higher Education*, 23, 3, 273–95.

Webster, D S (1985) 'Does research productivity enhance teaching?', *Educational Record*, 66, 60–63.

Chapter 4

Effect of Funding Council Policies on Teaching Quality

Lewis Elton

INTRODUCTION

There is increasing concern that the trend of the last few years which has put teaching in general, and pedagogic research and development in particular, higher on the agenda of higher education is being inadvertently reversed as a result of current policies of the Funding Councils. In an expanding higher education system and a deteriorating financial situation, such a reversal would lead to a deterioration in the quality of higher education which would rapidly become permanent. This chapter suggests a means within current funding policies by which this reversal could be halted, so as to give quality a chance of being maintained.

THE PRESENT SITUATION

To get hard evidence on any deterioration of teaching quality is not easy. In the current competitive climate, it is not in the interest of any university to admit to such deterioration, since it may adversely affect its ability to attract students. For a different reason, the Funding Councils too would appear to have a vested interest in hiding any deterioration, namely that it could be construed as being due to recent cut-backs in funding. It is significant that the first overt claim for such a deterioration has come in connection with the need of many students to work part-time during terms, which cuts into their study time (Targett, 1994). Not only does this lay the blame for any possible deterioration exclusively on the most vulnerable constituency in higher education, but it also allows an immediate suggestion as to how to remedy the situation, which again involves only students, namely to expect them to take on larger loans.

The evidence that has come from the Enterprise in Higher Education Initiative (EHE) is less about deterioration of teaching quality than about deterioration in the motivation and the effort that teachers are prepared to put into the kind of teaching innovation that is an essential part of EHE. This is affecting many of the most dedicated university teachers and it will in the longer run undoubtedly lead to a deterioration of teaching quality. Most of the evidence at this stage is inevitably largely anecdotal, in part at least because such dedicated teachers are naturally reluctant to admit to loss of motivation and effort. At the same time, such a situation rapidly becomes irreversible, if it is not remedied quickly, so that by the time that hard evidence is available, the damage has been done and is very hard to undo.

The most telling evidence can be found in the Annual Reports of EHE institutions over the years. Until about 1992, EHE was driven by enthusiasts who found the work immensely motivating and who felt that it was appreciated by their heads of departments. This gradually changed with the advent of the 1992 Research Assessment Exercise, which placed great stress on the production of publications. Increasingly staff were told that their departments could no longer afford great effort being put into teaching innovation and that priority number one was the production of at least two research papers by each member of staff. While this has never been put as crudely into EHE Annual Reports, it has become a constant refrain in discussions between EHE staff and the Higher Education Advisers (HEAs) of the Employment Department. More sanitized versions have then appeared in Annual Reports. The important point to note is that this phenomenon was never noticed during the earlier period of EHE, 1988–91; it became apparent to HEAs in 1992 and is now fully accepted by EHE institutions.

POSSIBLE CAUSES FOR THE OBSERVED DETERIORATION IN MOTIVATION AND EFFORT

The fact that the deterioration can be dated so neatly to coincide with the results of Funding Council pressures in the research area in itself does not establish a cause-and-effect relationship, but it does make a *prima facie* case for it. This is strengthened by the fact that it is not just an observed relationship, but one that has been explained by academic staff in the terms indicated. At the same time, there are related effects, due to current Funding Council policies and practices:

- There are real financial rewards in the research area. While the major rewards go to quite a small proportion of universities, often and very significantly referred to as 'elite' universities, at least some reward went to every university and a number of colleges of HE in the recent allocation. While the new universities received much less than the old universities, many received at least £1M and some more than £2M. This is new money, which was never available before, and it is free to be used within research, as each institution sees fit. There is nothing to correspond to this on the teaching side and the comparatively small sums available to institutions in such teaching development programmes as the Teaching and Learning Technology Programme (TLTP), etc, are firmly tied to particular projects.

- The rhetoric of the recent HEFCE Annual Report 1992–3 reinforces the imbalance between teaching and research. As regards teaching, 'the Council will recognise excellence in education in its funding decisions', but warns that in the first year 'there will be a need to be particularly cautious about the link between funding and an "excellent" grade'. I shall return to this point later, but in any case the reward mechanism, which consisted of an increase in student numbers with their associated financial support, is first, hardly a reward, second, not available to universities which for one reason or another are not in a position to expand, third, not available at present because of the capping of student numbers and fourth, not 'free' money in the way that research money is.

- In contrast, the section on research sends strong signals, which support the current belief among the less research-oriented institutions that their teaching-oriented value system may conflict with that of HEFCE. The quotation 'Universities and colleges are collectively the main national providers of research' appears to extend the research base to include even colleges of HE (Roehampton got £1.2M in the last allocation), and two of the four pictures, including the largest one, are from new universities, while only one is from one that can be described marginally as among the elite. The Report also refers to 'areas of high quality research effort in the PCFC sector and those previously funded by the DfE or local authorities'. The message that research is to be spread to all universities, and even colleges, is strong and clear. It contrasts unfortunately with what HEFCE officials say in private, namely that concentration of research will continue and get fiercer, so that many of those institutions which have received rewards in the current round may find themselves excluded in the next. But even if that should be the case, and to give such conflicting messages is both unfortunate and inefficient, no institution can lightly ignore the possibility of extra funds now, and only one, the University of Central England, has effectively done so.

- While the total sum for research in the current allocation has shown an increase over previous years, that for teaching continues to decrease at a rate of about 2 per cent per year per student.

● The effect of quality assessment is difficult to judge at this early stage, but there is some evidence that a disproportionate number of 'excellent' ratings is going to the old universities. The easiest explanation, that this reflects the true situation, is by no means the only one, and it is not even the most likely one, in view of the very different efforts that old and new universities have put into teaching in the past. More sophisticated explanations include:
  – assessors favour traditional teaching. This is strengthened by the way that the assessment concentrates on classroom practice. Much innovative teaching takes place outside classrooms and in situations in which students are not in direct contact with teachers;
  – it is obviously easier to achieve excellence in a traditional way; innovations always have their risks;
  – assessors are recruited from 'eminent' academics, and eminence is more usually associated with research than teaching excellence. Such academics would be more concerned with the *what* than the *how* of teaching, which again would favour the old universities;
  – in connection with this conjecture, Barnett (1994) reports on 'some reluctance among the older universities to release experienced members of staff'. It must not, however be assumed that assessors from the new universities are more sympathetic to innovative teaching methods; some anecdotal evidence indicates the opposite.

Clearly, this is one issue on which there is at present no certainty and on which more certainty is important to establish.

STRATEGIES FOR CREATING CHANGE

In a rapidly changing environment, universities inevitably are changing. The question that needs considering is the extent to which such change is of the universities' own making and the extent to which it is influenced by external factors, in particular funding policies. The rhetoric of the Funding Councils is that universities are independent bodies and that it is the task of the Funding Councils to encourage them to achieve excellence within the aims which they declare, but that it is not for the Funding Councils to question these aims. How far does this rhetoric correspond to the reality of the situation? An interesting light is thrown on this question by the very different ways that the Funding Councils and the EHE Initiative have been treating universities.

EHE has been quite open about being an agent of change and the important features in its change strategy appear to be the following:

- The Employment Department was prescriptive only in the broadest manner, but in this way provided a firm framework within which institutions – and indeed departments within institutions – could develop innovations. They initiated development plans which they then put to the Employment Department, for the latter to improve through dialogue and then to approve, before contracts were signed. This approach is radically different from the way that financial support is normally disbursed by government agencies.

- Once institutions had signed contracts, staff of the Employment Department continued to work with them. Contracts were reviewed and renewed annually and could be adjusted even during the year by mutual agreement. This work was done by a development manager and a higher education adviser, assigned to each institution, who worked as a team. Within the team, the development manager naturally had more of the task of ensuring that the contract was properly fulfilled and the higher education adviser more of the task of acting as a curriculum adviser, but in the best teams – and they were the rule rather than the exception – each of them did aspects of both.

- The Employment Department funding is for future activities and is dependent on being matched by corresponding support from institutions and employers, although the latter was allowed to be in kind. There was no insistence on matched funding in cash. This arrangement led to a far bigger contribution in kind than could ever have been obtained in cash through matched funding, which would in any event have been impossible to obtain. But much more importantly, the contribution in kind came largely from the time given by committed people, whose enthusiasm was an added bonus that it would not have been possible to quantify in cash terms.

What these strategies had in common was that they all relied on both carrot and stick but much more on carrot without ever doing wholly away with stick. This well-known prescription for successful change (Lewin, 1952) is far too rarely put into practice.

The strategies of the Funding Councils have been more covert and they may indeed deny that they are in the business of having a strategy. Nevertheless, I maintain that effectively they do have a strategy which can be analysed as follows in terms of the above three dimensions:

- The Funding Councils wholly eschew being prescriptive; indeed they explicitly deny their right to be so in deference to academic freedom. For the same reason, they do not engage in dialogue with universities. Unfortunately, such a complete absence of direction and of boundaries leaves universities insecure and leads in practice to convergent and even compliant planning across the university sector. In contrast, the firm boundaries of the EHE strategy and the initial dialogue fostered great variety within those boundaries in institutional proposals.

- The external assessment by the Funding Councils of the institutional self-assessment discourages honest self-evaluation, which is necessary for improvement, and the feedback after the assessment is resisted, as it is so intimately associated with financial penalties. In contrast, the dialogue and feedback in EHE continues throughout the contract. While the latter can be renegotiated at any time, it is reviewed annually, which provides the minimal sanction needed to safeguard against bad practice. Furthermore, the negotiation process gives security in experimentation and continues the process of institutional divergence.

- Rewards and penalties of the Funding Councils are made retrospectively, ie on the basis of the quality of work done. This encourages a conservative attitude and does not encourage support from other agencies. In contrast, EHE allocates funds on the basis of proposals for the future and makes the allocation conditional on other support being obtained. The difference between rewarding past excellence and encouraging future excellence is perhaps the most significant difference between the two funding methods.

In sum, although the Funding Councils do pursue a strategy and use both carrot and stick, the balance between the two is inflexible and far too heavily biased towards the stick. This inflexibility in fact extends to the strategy as a whole, maintaining a top-down relationship between Funding Councils and universities into the indefinite future and preventing a gradual transition to institutional independence.

THE QUESTION OF UNINTENDED CONSEQUENCES

As the Funding Councils effectively are agents of change, it becomes important to investigate the secondary consequences of their exchange strategies. These are an inevitable accompaniment of the desired primary consequences and they more often than not are deleterious (Elton, 1989). They also ter.d to last longer. A good example now accepted by

Professor Graeme Davies (1993), is the effect that the number of publications as a performance indicator for research excellence has had on publication production. The number of publications has increased out of all proportion to any conceivable increase in research activity, they have become repetitive and they have become shorter, so that what might previously have been one substantial piece of work, now appears broken up into separate papers. There is no evidence that any of this is due to an improvement, either quantitatively or qualitatively, in research effort; the only beneficiaries have been the publishers of journals, which have mushroomed. Whether similar effects will become apparent in teaching over the next few years it is too early to tell, but the auguries are not good. The proposed inclusion of performance indicators in quality assessment (for a warning, see Yorke, 1993), the use of rankings and league tables, and the intention for ever-finer divisions of rating, all are fruitful sources of wholly predictable, although presumably unintended, deleterious secondary consequences.

A PROPOSAL FOR A MORE EVEN TREATMENT OF RESEARCH AND TEACHING

It would probably be unrealistic in the present climate of opinion regarding the relative importance of teaching and research, to entertain the possibility of a genuinely level playing field, let alone one which is tilted towards teaching to provide affirmative action for the less prestigious. Neither is that necessary and the justification for that statement lies again in the EHE experience.

What the EHE experience has shown is that in every university that took part in the Initiative, there was a proportion of academic staff who wished to put their inventiveness and creativity into teaching rather than into research. This proportion was somewhere between 10 and 20 per cent, irrespective of the research or teaching orientation of the institution. It is for these that it is necessary to provide the level playing field and this is not impossible to achieve. In fact, what I am going to suggest is not a level playing field, but two separate playing fields, one for those who strive for research excellence and one for those who strive for teaching excellence. Many will want to switch from one to the other at different times of their careers, a few will want to play on both at the same time. The maintenance of the teachers' playing field will however be very significantly less costly than that of the researchers, not only because teaching innovation can be legitimately considerably less expensive than much research, but also because for a long time to come the number of players on the field will be very much smaller. All this comes directly out of the EHE experience.

The excellence that I am referring to is very different from the kind of excellence that quality assessment is trying to identify. It is the excellence of an individual or a small group of staff, and only occasionally that of whole departments, in pedagogic research and development, and the reward for such excellence should lie in support for future activities. In all this it is much closer to the concept of excellence that is used in the Research Assessment Exercise and is, of course, wholly in line with the way that EHE has acted. On the other hand, the financial scale of what is needed is very much the EHE scale and not that of the Funding Council Research Assessment .

So why should such work not be simply included as a small addition to the Research Assessment Exercise? Even where such work might fit the rules of the Funding Councils for inclusion, and this would rarely be the case, there are difficulties. It does not fit readily into the preconceptions of education departments as to what constitutes fundamental research and rarely takes place in such departments but usually in subject-specific departments. On the other hand, it would be quite inappropriate for it to be judged by the subject research panels, whose expertise is not of course in the pedagogic research of their subject. A far more appropriate solution arises from the fact that such work is almost always strategic or even tactical research and therefore does not qualify for research funding under the Councils' rules, which say that such research should be funded by the beneficiaries of the research. However, in this case the beneficiaries are of course the Funding Councils themselves. As the major funders of higher education, whose money will be used more effectively as the result of such research, they should fund it not as a disinterested party, but as the major interested party. Some such funding already occurs, eg through the TLTP programme, and this should be continued. But what is needed in addition is a much more open teaching research and development fund, in which the initiative is taken by the researchers and not by the Councils. Such a Fund would not have to be large, initially probably no more than about £25M, although since its intention would be to encourage academics to go in for research and development in higher education pedagogy, one would hope that it would have to grow soon.

Finally, I suggest that there may well be another problem that faces the Funding Councils in connection with pedagogic research. It is that such research is at present very little understood by most people outside those who are practising it, for the simple reason that such people rarely if ever have had any pedagogic training, let alone carried out pedagogic research. To the extent that this is likely to apply also to the staff of the Funding Councils, they should recognize that some such training might be as appropriate for them as it is for all academic staff.

CONCLUSION

The purpose of this chapter was to find a way within the current policies of the Funding Councils by which research and development in teaching could be given an appropriate funding mechanism. The conclusion is that this is best achieved by linking such funding to the direct interest which the Funding Councils have in the improvement of teaching, rather than by incorporating this activity within the Funding Councils' Research Assessment.

REFERENCES

Barnett, R (1994) *Assessment of Quality in Higher Education: A review and an evaluation*, University of London : Centre for Higher Education Studies.

Davies, G (1993) 'Quality assessment methodology: how it addresses employer education links', Second Quality in Higher Education Seminar, Warwick University, December.

Elton, L (1989) 'Accountability in higher education: the danger of unintended consequences', *Higher Education*, 17, 377–90.

Elton, L (1994) 'Enterprise in Higher Education – an agent for change', in Knight, P (ed.) *University-wide Change: Staff and curriculum development*, SEDA Paper 83.

Lewin, K (1952) *Field Theory in Social Science*, London: Tavistock.

Targett, S (1994) 'Standards threat as students moonlight', *Times Higher Education Supplement*, 4 February, p.1.

Yorke, M (1993) 'Siamese twins? Performance indicators in the service of accountability and enhancement', Annual Conference of the Society for Research into Higher Education, University of Sussex, December.

Chapter 5

Research, Teaching and Learning: A Symbiotic Relationship

David Garnett and Roy Holmes

INTRODUCTION

Traditionally, higher education has been seen to have two broad functions: research and learning. To use the language of contemporary educational philosophy, the academy is concerned with the production and reproduction of knowledge; it both generates and disseminates understanding and ideas.

The interrelating of research and learning has always been the primary role of the university. A wide range of organizations and people engage in research – government departments, firms, research institutes, individuals – but what traditionally separates university research from other research is the academy's commitment to make open and public the knowledge and understanding to which it lays claim. It has a commitment to 'profess'. A member of a university is expected not only to practise an art or science but also to act as a 'professor' of knowledge. So, even in the title we bestow on senior academics there is a semantic commitment to teach.

It is worthy of note that the words 'professor' and 'profession' come from the same root (the Latin *professus*, to confess). The word 'profession' was originally used as a noun meaning 'the act of professing', in particular the act of vowing to bind oneself to a religious order. It was then extended to embrace other callings or vocations, especially an occupation involving high educational or technical qualification – which brings us back to the key role of the higher education academy.

A RANKED SYSTEM

As we move from a bifurcated to an ostensibly unified system of higher education, we need to be clear about the relationship between research and learning. In the old 'polytechnic sector', the CNAA position was straightforward, if not altogether clear. It was argued (rather vaguely) that undergraduate and postgraduate teaching needs to be underpinned by research. This position implies a certain hierarchical relationship between teaching and researching – 'we research in order to teach'. However, the ostensibly unified system of higher education may, in fact, be becoming divided in terms of a new hierarchy that will establish different 'classes' of university, differentiated by their contrasting research/learning relationships.

Some universities may become predominantly teaching institutions, with a research programme designed to underpin the delivery of the curriculum. Others will be identified as centres for 'quality research' and will, as a result, be funded differently. Such a divide implies a hierarchy of institutions with 'first division' research institutes at its pinnacle and 'third division' teaching colleges at its base. Such a picture challenges the traditional view that, within each academy, there needs to be a balanced, symbiotic relationship between researching and professing.

It may be argued that a top-rank academic best professes through publications rather than through lecturing and tutoring. Indeed, as Parsons (1968) intimated, the professionalization of the academic in the twentieth century has meant that reputations are established in national and international research-centred forums rather than in locally-defined pedagogic arrangements. This modern view of 'professional' scholarship tends to regard teaching as an unfortunate or unnecessary interruption in the academic's 'real' work, which is to complete a piece of contract research or to prepare an article to be published in a learned journal or a paper to be presented at a conference of peers. In this vision, professors profess to professors and their ideas only find a wider audience if and when their research findings and ideas leak out of the research community's confines, by being picked up by a different group of 'lesser' academics, who spend most of their time teaching (recontextualizing and transmitting the work of others). It would appear that some are destined to produce while others are destined to reproduce; the hierarchy is clear and the divide is established.

This picture of a ranked system of higher education may not be true, or it may not be true yet, or it may never be true in the simplistic way in which it has been presented here; or it may become in some sense true and be justifiable. In any event, we need to know whether, or to what extent it is, or will be true, if we are to make any sensible suggestions about the respective roles of teaching and research in universities. The fact that it is believed to be true has already produced questions of significance about what constitutes a university. Can a university exist without any research? Is there a critical mass of research that needs to exist in order to be a university? Should everyone do research? Should everyone teach? What counts as research? Such questions lead to others about the categorization of educational knowledge, the privileging of institutions in terms of research funding, the selecting and allocating of students to subject areas and institutions, the appointment and development of university staff, and so on.

A NEW EDUCATIONAL FRAMEWORK

The significance of these questions has been heightened by the national drive to open university education to a wider range of students. As total student numbers rise, other questions present themselves. These questions are not so much about what constitutes a university as about how a university should operate. The MacFarlane Report (1993) identifies four questions that are of pressing importance.

- How can high quality environments to support learning be created and maintained at a time when numbers are expected to increase dramatically?

- What role has technology to play in creating such environments?

- How can an increasing effectiveness and the containment of costs be reconciled with a high quality of learning experience?

- How can the status of teaching, both as a professional activity and as a sphere for research, be raised in the higher education sector?

We would argue that these questions highlight further urgent problems about the relationship between learning and research. In particular they point to the potential dilemma that results from a recognition that students need to work in an environment that is impregnated with a culture of research while their tutors are finding it increasingly difficult to find the time and resources to maintain a viable research programme. Although Ball (1992) said that 'teaching and research are as inseparable as wool and mutton on a sheep-farm' there is an increasing tendency to speak of the 'research community' as a distinctive group within the university.

The MacFarlane argument is that we now need research about higher education itself and, in particular, how to cope with large numbers of students without sacrificing the quality of the learning experience. As part of this we need to develop a clear understanding of the role of university research in an educational environment of mass education in which tensions between teaching and researching will certainly arise as a result of a diminishing unit of resource.

In particular, we need to identify the symbiotic relationship between research and teaching by clarifying the following set of related questions.

- What are the aims of higher education?
- How can research support learning?
- How can teaching help develop research?

CONTRIBUTION OF RESEARCH TO TEACHING AND LEARNING

It is accepted that research makes a significant contribution to teaching and learning by underpinning the curricula of honours and postgraduate degrees. Recent work on the application of research in teaching by Glew (1992) has indicated that research can transform the teaching/learning experience. For the teacher it creates confidence, promotes self-esteem and releases motivating power during class contact. For the student it provides the opportunity to engage in the skill of enquiry and critique, which is a pivotal experience in higher education; it also gives them exposure to the current state of the art in a particular field of study. In addition, it provides staff with a framework to develop a range of teaching/learning inputs, including up-to-date teaching material and research-related projects and workshops. Moreover, it often provides the opportunity for staff to remain in touch with industry and practice and thereby better understand the requirements and pressures of the world of affairs. Furthermore, students engage in absorbing projects and case studies, which are seen to be relevant and up-to-date. These benefits are shown in Figure 5.1. We now need to stress that the research/teaching relationship is a two-way process.

CONTRIBUTION OF TEACHING AND LEARNING TO RESEARCH

The symbiotic relationship between research and teaching creates an environment in which the researcher has to plan the presentation of the research carefully; simple conceptual models may have to be prepared for teaching purposes. The presentation of such models and the discussion of the research in the classroom may expose research weaknesses. This leads to the modification of the presentation and, in so doing, helps the researcher to think through and improve the explanation of the research. Undergraduate students often think in divergent ways and ask

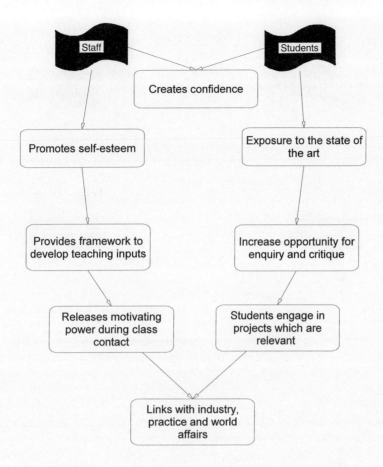

Figure 5.1 *The benefits of research in teaching and learning*

questions about peripheral or related concepts, which the researcher may not have considered – see Figure 5.2.

At postgraduate level, the input from students can be dramatic, particularly in a studio or workshop environment. In this context, the implications of the research methodology or output can come under some pressure. This is particularly so with part-time postgraduate students who are in professional practice. In a recent workshop with postgraduate students, a research project was used to illustrate how management of resources could be optimized. The methodology for the optimization became the centre of a prolonged discussion in which the two workshop leaders, both keen researchers, had to concede that an important management issue raised by the students had been under-valued in the conceptual model – see Figure 5.3 for the process. The issue was of such

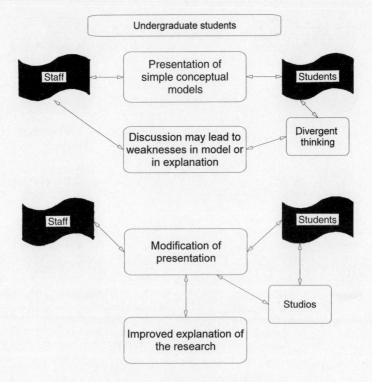

Figure 5.2   *The benefits of teaching and learning in research*

significance that the researchers have not only modified the model but are considering mounting a second research project on that one issue alone.

This serves as an illustration of the dynamic nature of the relationship and also makes the point that there is an opportunity for the teacher/researcher to test ideas and concepts at very low cost. Some groups of postgraduate students represent a wide constituency, have an extremely high corporate potential and provide their input freely. To assemble a 'think tank' with the same breadth of experience would take a great deal of effort, and could be costly.

TEACHING AND RESEARCH AS COMPLEMENTARY FORMS OF SCHOLARSHIP

When we consider curriculum development we should never lose sight of the fact that research is an aspect of scholarship that enthuses the student and creates expectations, which improves the esteem of the teacher; but

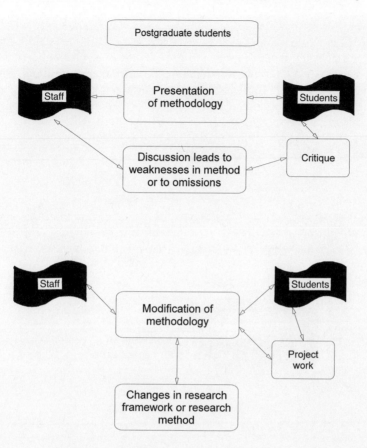

Figure 5.3   *Benefits of teaching and learning in research*

more than that, it provides the opportunity for enquiring minds to explore concepts, to probe methodologies and, perhaps, to challenge the thinking that goes into many research programmes. Undergraduates should not be deprived of teachers who are engaged in the production of knowledge, and postgraduates will give little credibility to teachers who have no research interests. In the modern academy, research is universally accepted as a form of scholarship. Following Rice (1992), we now wish to argue for the re-establishment of teaching as a valued form of scholarship.

Having to integrate research into the teaching curriculum is a good way of clarifying research concepts and making explicit their wider implications. As Rice argues, the scholarship of teaching has a distinctive *synoptic capacity*, that is, 'the ability to draw the strands of a field together in a way that provides both coherence and meaning, to place what is known in context and open the way for connections to be made between the knower and the known'. The teacher/researcher draws on data, ideas or theories taken from the research project and presents them in such a way that creates coherence and meaning both for teacher and individual students. Given that students bring their own perceptions and experiences into the pedagogic activity, individual coherences and meanings will fail to be conterminous. It is this tension that has a potential for transforming the research thinking. Figure 5.4 highlights the synoptic capacity of pedagogic activity.

CONCLUSION

Higher education is concerned with both the production and reproduction of knowledge. University staff are expected to be involved in the

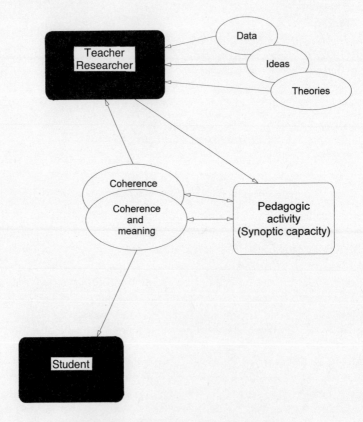

Figure 5.4   *Teaching – a form of scholarship*

former by means of research. This knowledge needs to be disseminated to students and to do this effectively the researcher must be involved in teaching. Investigations into the application of teaching and learning indicate many positive features for both the student and the teacher. However, little if any research has been carried out into the benefits that teaching has on research. Our experience indicates that the benefits are legion; the researcher finds a willing and often able audience with whom to expound and develop ideas and clarify concepts. It provides a very cost-effective way in which to test for implications and applicability. Research and teaching are not in conflict – the relationship is two-way and genuinely symbiotic; by combining the two activities it is often possible to create a product that has a value that is significantly greater than the sum of the parts.

REFERENCES

Ball, C (1992) 'Teaching and research', in Wiston, T and Geiger, R (eds), *Research and Higher Education*, SRHE and OU Press.

CSUP (1992) *Teaching and Learning in an Expanding Higher Education System, Report of a Working Party of the Committee of Scottish University Principals*, Edinburgh: CSUP.

Glew, G (1992) 'Research and the quality of degree teaching – with special reference to consumer and leisure studies degree courses', *CNAA Project Report 38*, October, CNAA.

Parsons, T (1968) 'Professions', in Sills, D L (ed.) *International Encyclopaedia of the Social Sciences*, Basingstoke: Macmillan.

MacFarlane, A (1993) *Teaching and Learning in an Expanded Higher Education Section*, HEFCE.

Rice, R E (1992) 'Towards a broader conception of scholarship: the American context' in Wiston, T and Geiger, R, *Research and Higher Education*, SRHE and OU Press.

Chapter 6

The Importance of Applied Research

Peter Smith and Marshall Elliott

This chapter discusses the current and future importance of applied research, as opposed to basic or strategic research. This subject has become of increasing importance in recent years due to several reasons. In particular, recent commercial and financial pressures have meant that those undertaking any research of any form must, more and more, justify the relevance and worth of their work to the funding bodies or companies who are financing that work. This has, by necessity, resulted in a much more applied and practical orientation to many research projects.

The recent government White Paper on the future of science and engineering research (HMSO, 1993) has also focused upon the importance of industry/academia collaboration. Also, the research programmes which are funded by the European Union (e.g. ESPRIT, BRITE/EURAM) are becoming more and more industrially oriented and require the partners within a project consortium to consider the exploitation potential of the results of their research.

The new universities have, from their inception in the 1960s, approached their undergraduate and postgraduate work from a practical and vocational viewpoint. This, coupled with the way in which they have been traditionally funded, has meant that they are used to working on industrially and commercially relevant research projects. This applied research has also carried through into the highly vocational nature of their degree and diploma courses.

This chapter summarizes the above issues and discusses the impact that they are having upon the UK. research community. The major issues are illustrated by considering the two subject areas with which the authors are most familiar: information technology (IT) and business studies.

BACKGROUND

In recent years, academics have been required increasingly to justify their research. It is no longer enough to undertake blue skies research simply because it is of interest, or on the basis that it may lead to more practical benefits to industry or the community at large in the longer term. Research Councils, the European Community and industry/commerce are asking for and, indeed, requiring the demonstration of more tangible benefits within a much shorter timescale. This inevitably means that researchers are having to undertake research of a much more applied nature.

It can, of course, be argued that this applied edge is of great benefit to both the academic community and to UK and European industry. Ultimately this should feed into, and benefit, the UK and European economy. But is the movement to such applied research also stifling and impeding many important research activities which would reach fruition in a much longer time scale? In order, at least partially, to address the above question this chapter considers the state of current research in, and the implications for, two diverse areas: IT and business studies.

IT RESEARCH

There have been in recent years a large number of UK and EU initiatives which will fund applied research. A selection of these are summarized below.

ALVEY

Although the ALVEY programme has now concluded, its importance is such that no review of applied research in IT would be complete without mentioning it. The ALVEY programme for advanced information technology was launched in 1982 as a direct response to the Japanese Fifth Generation Programme. The ALVEY programme encompassed many different aspects of IT, and the budget for the programme was around £350M over a period of five years. It was based upon the concept of promoting joint collaborative research projects between academia and industry. The ALVEY programme succeeded in stimulating and promoting research into all areas of IT by the funding of collaborative research projects, workshops, conferences and technology transfer and development clubs. This resulted in many exciting advances and helped to forge real links between industrial organizations and academic institutions. Unfortunately, subsequent funding was not provided at a similarly high level and hence many research ideas and prototype systems were not able to progress into exploitable products.

The Manufacturing Intelligence Programme

The DTI mounted the Manufacturing Intelligence Programme in 1989 with the aim of increasing managers' awareness of how IT can benefit their business. The programme was designed to encourage, and fund, research in the area and was open to industrial companies, academic institutions, software specialists and research and development organizations. Manufacturing Intelligence is defined as the use of software to solve problems in the manufacturing and process industries. The programme, which closed in 1993, offered the following research and technology transfer initiatives:

- a number of collaborative projects funded by the programme and run by industry and academia;

- awards which were given annually to those projects/products which were deemed to demonstrate excellence in the application of knowledge-based techniques in the manufacturing and process industries. Previous finalists for this award have included: LISA – a knowledge-based system for configuring fire protection systems; DIPLOMA – a knowledge-based system for the support of repair and overhaul functions in the aerospace industry; and a system for the intelligent assembly of telephone directories;

- regional clubs which were set up by the programme across the UK to discuss Manufacturing Intelligence issues, mount seminars and promote technology transfer.

Research with Europe

Any large funding for IT research in the UK is likely to have a European dimension in the future. In 1988, the British Minister for Industry and Consumer Affairs commented on the role of the ESPRIT (European Strategic Programme of Research in Information Technology) programme:

> Britain is part of Europe and is working with other member states to secure the single market. This surely means it is right to put emphasis on European collaborations. European-scale effort is often needed when large investments will be required for the research itself or for the subsequent production and marketing of the product. ESPRIT provides the opportunity for both our companies and our universities to participate in research on a European scale and to develop the commercial relationship that will be needed.

ESPRIT has provided funding for a large number of multinational collaborative projects involving academia and commercial companies since the programme began in the early 1980s. The ESPRIT programme has thus been of enormous significance in creating a truly collaborative community of European researchers, developers and users.

Current trends

The recent government White Paper on research (HMSO, 1993) concluded that the UK needs to develop stronger partnerships with and between the science and engineering communities, industry and the research charities. It continued, 'Science, engineering and technology are critical to our future well-being; we must all work together to make sure that they contribute fully to realising the country's potential'. All of this points to a move towards more practical, applied, industry-led research in the field of IT.

BUSINESS STUDIES

This section poses the question: are business schools engaging sufficiently in research that leads to direct improvements in the performance of private and public sector organizations? Certainly it is the belief of the authors that there is an urgent need for academics in higher education to be less self-indulgent in pursuing research that has no direct application and to become much more aware and focused on the needs of the wider business community.

Perhaps much of the problem with business research stems from the development of many of the current management research groups from social science research communities in academic departments, before the emergence of the modern business schools. Certainly the culture (and resulting 'jargon') of management research reflects this background, and has very little in common with the approach to applied research made in the areas of science and technology. Another problem for research is that in the make-up of a typical business school there tends to be a combination of practitioner lecturers and traditional academics. While this undoubtedly provides a good educational experience for students, the practitioners tend to focus on consultancy activity while research is left to the traditional academics, many of whom are remote from the real needs of the business community.

What is needed in order to face the challenges of the new century are business schools that are much more reactive to the needs of industry and commerce, and which can effectively mobilize and manage large-scale interdisciplinary research projects. Much closer links between business and science and technology are needed, as are more collaborative links with organizations outside academia. The proposed fourth framework programme of European Union activities in the field of research, due for implementation from 1994, identifies a number of problems that have arisen from previous research programmes due to the lack of take-up by industry of the new technologies that have been developed. As a result more business-related research activities have been designed into themes for the new programme, which afford new opportunities for business schools to link into, and play a vital role in the support of, technology-based research.

The ESRC (Economic and Social Research Council) Industrial Links programme and the EPSRC (Engineering and Physical Sciences Research Council) Teaching Company scheme are two further examples of collaborative opportunities that can assist business research in moving forwards with applied research. It is noteworthy that the recently published government White Paper on a strategy for science, engineering and technology (HMSO, 1993) also makes reference to the need for closer links between science, technology and business, including the need for the development of new postgraduate courses in the management of technology.

Unfortunately, the HEFCE (Higher Education Funding Council of England) research assessment (and thus funding) systems need considerable amendments if support is to be provided to research teams that are responsive to the needs of the business community and therefore the performance of the economy as a whole. Further pressure needs to be applied by other funding bodies to affect the necessary changes in academia.

A COUNTER-ARGUMENT

A recent study carried out by Wendy Faulkner at the University of Edinburgh's Research Centre for Social Sciences, Jacqueline Senker of the Science Policy Research Unit, University of Sussex and Lea Velho, now at the University of Campinas in Brazil, gave an alternative view that the current government emphasis on relevance and near-market science and technology in the publicly-funded research sector is misplaced (Faulkner and Senker, 1993).

The study, backed by the ESRC, explored public-private research links by investigating three new and promising fields of advanced technology: pharmaceutical biotechnology, advanced engineering ceramics and parallel computing. The aim was to explore how these industries interact with public sector research.

The report concludes that public research contributes greatly to innovation by training qualified scientists and engineers and by thus providing a source of new knowledge, upon which more applied research can be based and grow. The authors further conclude that the importance to industry of such basic research which is currently taking place in many government laboratories and academic departments confirms that it should not be sacrificed for what is seen to be more relevant and near-market work. Of the three sectors investigated, the research team found that biotechnology is the only field where government-funded research contributes more knowledge to corporate research and development than that achieved by links between companies themselves. In all three areas, they found that public science contributes to corporate research, design and development.

DISCUSSION

There are a number of important issues relating to applied research which have been touched on in this chapter. The first of these concerns definition of terms, or more precisely, the distinction between applied research, strategic research and consultancy.

The distinction between the applied end of research and consultancy is a particularly grey area. A consultancy project can often also be classed as an applied research project, and consultancy can often spin off into research or vice-versa. Ownership of the results may be a key issue. That is, in the case of consultancy, it is usually clear that the company which has paid for the work owns the rights to the work. In research, of course, it may not be so clear. For example, in large collaborative projects the project consortium may jointly own the rights to the results of the work.

When considering the difference between strategic and applied research, strategic research has an application in the longer term, whereas applied research has an application now. Strategic research may be market-oriented (ie, you know what the market will be).

All of this begs the question as to whether there is such a thing as pure research. It is often difficult to think of research which has no possible application at all. So even so-called pure research may have an application in the (much) longer term.

We have alluded to the fact that there appears to be a growing move towards the applied aspects of research, and that the recent science White Paper strengthens this move. Does this then suggest that all of the UK Research Councils will move more towards applied research? This certainly appears to be the case. The European Commission has already moved this way. The European Commission is not allowed to fund product development but it is keen to fund projects which will produce 'prototype' products, which can then be exploited shortly after completion of the project. This is, of course, sensible in terms of getting the best 'value for money': there have been far too many large projects which have not produced any real results.

Because of the pressures on industry, this is also the case for industry-funded research. This means that research is becoming more industrial, product-led and market-driven and that this is forcing milestones, deliverables and more tight and careful project management upon researchers.

Will this limit academic freedom? Will it restrict important ideas? There does appear to be a conflict here. On the one hand there seems to be a push towards applied research; on the other, there seems to be limited funding available for such research and a suggestion that industry should itself fund the research. Unfortunately, British industry supports research to a far lesser extent than other countries. For example, in the USA industry often gives money to a university to do research with very few 'strings attached'. This seem unlikely to happen in the UK, given the current state of British industry and manufacturing in particular.

The authors believe that it is still important that a significant amount of pure research continues to be funded, this is also borne out by the study of Faulkner and Senker. Otherwise, the UK will fall further behind those countries which are more forward-thinking and do fund 'blue skies' research. It also seems likely that 'global' research will become more and more commonplace in the future; that is, multi-continental collaboration which involves partnerships between, for example, Europe, the USA and Japan will emerge in the coming decades.

The experience of researchers in the areas of IT and business at the University of Sunderland is that applied research is becoming more important. However, this has not caused us any great problems. We are used to working with industry and commerce, and to applying our research ideas to the solution of real-world problems. Further, we are also used to working on large collaborative projects with several partners from different countries.

CONCLUSIONS

Although the importance of applied research is without question, the authors do feel that there remains a role for more strategic and pure research. However, it is certain the level of funding available for such research will decrease in the future. The highly competitive market place in which the research community is now operating will continue to add an applied edge to much of the research which will be funded in the future. However, this can, in the longer term, only benefit industry, commerce and society in general.

ACKNOWLEDGEMENTS

The authors wish to thank those delegates who attended their session at the SEDA conference for their extremely useful contributions, some of which have been included in this chapter.

REFERENCES

Faulkner, W and Senker, J (1993) 'Making sense of diversity: Public-private sector research linkage in three technologies', *Research Policy*.

HMSO (1993) *Realising Our Potential: A strategy for science, engineering and technology*, London: Her Majesty's Stationery Office.

Patel, K (1993) 'Innovation needs pure research', *Times Higher Education Supplement*, 15 October.

Chapter 7

On Improving Learning Processes

Frank Walkden

INTRODUCTION

The thinking underlying the ideas in this chapter was prompted by a chance remark by a colleague that some people were good at making things happen, with the implication that others had less capability (or interest) in this direction. Subsequent discussions about possible reasons for this, which obviously will not be simple cause-and-effect relationships, led to the idea that one might usefully examine cases of people who have in a sense controlled events in some way and in some context, in order to see if some common ideas emerge. For the purposes of this chapter, those with no interest in shaping events, and who for this or any other reason may be classified as being less capable will be referred to as type A. This group may well be more numerous than the other category which here will be identified as type B. In addition, behaviour associated with each of these types, ie not making (or making) things happen in some context will be referred to as type A (or type B) behaviour respectively.

Cases considered in this chapter are: an entrepreneur, a group of students associated with a project designed to develop learning skills, and a researcher.

CASE COMMENTS

Introduction to case comments

Comments on cases are selective. They bring out points relevant to the present discussion rather than attempting to be complete in any sense. All the cases are ones with which the writer has been close enough to obtain an appreciation of underlying processes in some depth. Bias resulting from this is offset partially by the coverage of behaviour in different contexts which is facilitated by this approach.

The entrepreneur is a close relative with whom the writer has interacted in developing competence (the writer's) in business; the group of students was one that the writer worked with some years ago on a project to learn about the nature of expertise in learning; the researcher comments are based on the writer's own experience first as an apprentice learning how to do research, then as an independent researcher and latterly as a teacher of research methodologies through research supervision.

The entrepreneur

The entrepreneur was responsible for starting three businesses which are still trading and which between them employ about 120 people. One of the businesses was in a group of so-called superleague companies identified in a study by 3i, the venture capital company, because it had attained an exceptionally high rate of growth over a two-year period in the 1970s.

The entrepreneur had no obvious mentor or teacher; he acquired type B behaviour through his own efforts with a degree of trial and error; success followed a failed first attempt to start a business. He had a role model. He built and used a network of contacts which provided support. He had well-developed models of processes and situations which he used to guide actions, although he would not have been able to describe these models in words. Consequently he was not very successful in teaching others to follow and do much of what he was able to do himself. He tended to exhibit type A behaviour in contexts other than business.

The student group

The students involved in the learning skills project had all failed A-level examinations, some rather badly with an O-level pass or a grade U. However, subsequently out of six involved at the time, five have gone on to obtain a degree in mathematics. The students were introduced to a group of A-level teachers who were involved in a training programme organized by an LEA adviser who had been monitoring the student project. The teachers decided that the students were doing for themselves that which the teachers did for their students.

The students had a guide, and attained type B behaviour in the context of learning mathematics through a trial and error process after an initial failure. They had the benefit of a limited network environment consisting of their own peer group and a monitoring group which visited the project three times a year. They developed a mental model of the processes that they were using, but could not describe it well and were not very effective in helping other people to learn how to do what they were doing. Under direction some of them developed type B behaviour in learning contexts other than the primary one of improving mathematics learning skills.

The researcher

The researcher learned his trade in a then newly-emerging field of computational fluid dynamics. This involved convergence of disciplines of mathematics and numerical analysis, engineering mechanics and computing science. The aim of the work was to produce robust and accurate computational methods which could be used to support engineering design by facilitating reductions in the amount of expensive wind-tunnel experimentation that would otherwise be needed. For technical reasons, several serial modelling processes were involved and tracking down explanations of differences between theoretical and experimental results required formulation and comparison and refinement of conceptual models of physical, mathematical and computational processes. Progress resulted from insights gained through activities of this kind supported by numerical experiments designed to test particular hypotheses.

The researcher had a number of supervisors over the period in which he developed competence in research. He developed type B abilities slowly over a period of about nine years. He had the benefit of a network of contacts including peers and internationally-known experts. He developed a conceptual model of the research process which resulted in a high degree of unconscious competence in carrying out research of the type that was close to practice and involved the development and testing of concepts as part of the process of producing new insights that provided advances in knowledge. Through reflection on the process of developing competence and the difficulties encountered, which were due in part to the multi-disciplinary character of the research, a conceptual model of the skill development process was developed as well. This model was used consciously by the researcher in supervising research workers and helping them to develop their research skills.

Case discussion

The cases outlined indicate the importance of network connections; that type B behaviour can be transferred by individuals to contexts other than those in which they are learned, but that this is not natural and the ease with which it can be done may depend on whether or not a conscious process was used; that type B behaviour is acquired rather than innate; that the ability to teach others depends on ability to describe the mental models and processes being used.

Experience in areas covered by the cases outlined above suggests that a generalized research model and a general skill development process with potential for teaching people how to acquire type B characteristics in a variety of contexts could be developed. The contexts in which these methods might usefully be applied include development of independence and related investigatory skills in learning.

GENERAL CONCEPTUAL MODELS

Introduction to models

Outline descriptions of some elements of a general research activity model, a research skill development model and of one part of a traditional lecturing process are given here. The activity and skill models are a first attempt to describe general processes related to type B behaviour and how it may be acquired in multiple contexts with transfer of experience from one context to another.

Elements of a research activity model

Essential elements are:

- a knowledge base
- an appropriate set of skills and techniques
- a network of contacts
- a high degree of self-confidence
- the ability to ask and answer significant questions as part of the process of resolving issues.

The research skill development process

The novice is deficient in every one of the areas listed above and has to depend on the knowledge, experience and contacts of a supervisor.
Elements of the development model include:

- awareness of the kinds of barriers to progress in developing capability which arise in practice
- knowledge of ways in which each type of barrier may best be understood and removed

- formation of process views of the ways in which researchers (including the supervisor) work
- development of models of the activity process and the skill development process.

A teaching model

The model described here relates to lecturing which, of course, is a small though important part of the teaching process. A set of lectures (lessons in school) is designed to communicate a complete set of ideas which, in mathematics at least, will enable a student to perform some task, for example, solve a problem. After a lecture, a student will typically be given some problems for practice with the new ideas. Assuming necessary prerequisite knowledge a lecturer will use his or her expert skills and knowledge to develop ideas, putting them forward in an ordered way. The analogy of building a brick wall suggests itself. The bricks represent ideas and the interlocking arrangement represents the systematic development of connections between ideas necessary to produce a larger structure.

The 'brick wall' model breaks down in two situations. One of these is when prerequisite knowledge is missing. This prevents a proper understanding of the new ideas and leads to a 'symbol juggling' approach to solving problems, ie, manipulating symbols with no reference to any underlying theoretical justification for the action taken. This inevitably leads to stress, underachievement and ultimately to a situation where a student can proceed no further because the memorizing burden becomes intolerable. A second situation in which the expert-presenter approach breaks down is when there is no expert because the situation encountered is new to everyone; these cases arise in the real world, for example in industry where a company has to work in new ways or introduce new processes for which experts are not available.

An alternative to a sequential 'brick wall building approach' is one in which learning is incremental on several fronts and hence is essentially parallel. In this approach the emphasis is on gaining some experience and connecting ideas as necessary to fill gaps in knowledge (which are one of the outcomes of sequential knowledge that assumes prerequisite knowledge). An analogy for this approach is building a jigsaw puzzle; in this approach a framework (the straight and corner pieces) is erected and ideas (irregular pieces) are examined and connected together in order to construct a meaningful set of ideas (the whole or a part of the picture).

Two points in favour of this approach are that the methodology is more appropriate to the present requirements of employers, and that the approach offers scope for improving access without compromising standards. However, the approach can succeed only if students can be led to develop the type B research-oriented skills necessary for independent learning and investigatory capability.

Methods of facilitating this, that is independence and investigatory skills for learning, could possibly be developed by adapting general formalized approaches to training based on ideas outlined earlier.

DISCUSSION AND CONCLUSIONS

Issues

In this chapter it is suggested that the relationship between development of learning capability and development of research capability is a close one in that methods of training for one can be utilized for the other. Issues that need to be resolved include consideration of questions such as: can the research training process traditionally tailored to the requirements of individuals be adapted to deal with class-sized groups? If not, can individual support be provide economically and if so how?

Questions of this kind will need to be resolved through practical in-line trials. Provision of finance for research and development is a further issue. How much will be needed and how will it be provided?

Relationships to other work

The ideas presented in this chapter have been developed mainly from practical experiences of the writer, colleagues and students. They relate closely to ideas presented by Schön (1983). He argues the need for professionals who can adapt their techniques as necessary to deal with real problems in an appropriate way rather than persevering with inappropriate methods because no alternative is available. Such adaptation is essentially in-line research, but vocational education and training procedures will need changing to ensure that practitioners develop the necessary skills. Other work by Senge (1990), Schein (1993) and by Dorothy Leonard-Barton (1992) indicates the kind of organizations in which workers may be required to participate in the future. Here again there is an emphasis on investigative and process-orientated learning.

CONCLUSIONS

If research skills are to be taught more widely with a view to their use in developing independence and investigatory skills for enhancing learning capability, then a sound theoretical basis for instruction and training will be an essential prerequisite. Some evidence supporting the case for moving in the direction of research-oriented learning has been presented and a possible approach to developing a supporting theory has been suggested.

Able learners learn more quickly and need less support than others. Thus the overall gains that would follow from systematic improvement of the learning capability of individuals are so great that investment now to determine how the gains can be realized in practice would be amply repaid.

REFERENCES

Leonard-Barton, D (1992) 'The factory as a learning laboratory', *Sloan Management Review*, Fall.

Schein, E H (1993) 'How can organisations learn faster? The challenge of the green room', *Sloan Management Review*, Winter.

Schön. D A (1983) *The Reflective Practitioner*, London: Maurice Temple Smith.

Senge, P (1990) *The Fifth Discipline*, New York: Doubleday.

SECTION TWO

IDEAS IN PRACTICE

Chapter 8

Competent Research –
Running Brook or Stagnant Pool?

Phil Race

INTRODUCTION

For far too long there have been tensions between 'academic research'
and 'student-centred teaching and learning'. These tensions have been
exacerbated by the apparent conflicts between research and teaching, for
example the emphasis on research publications both in selection procedures for new appointments and in promotion criteria for existing
staff.

The aim of the workshop upon which this chapter is based was to
attempt to tease out the broad competences which underpin good-quality
research. With non-completion rates in PhD research at around 50 per
cent in some disciplines, it is timely to identify the competences that
really count in research. These competences may fall into various
categories of differing 'worth', including those relating to:

● research methodology;

● successful publication of research findings;

●
● successful research into teaching and learning processes and practices;

● successfully turning the outcomes of good teaching developments
   into 'the right kinds' of published research.

The comparative metaphor 'running brook versus stagnant pool' has
been used to compare those active in research from those who concentrate on teaching – but it can be argued that the real 'running brook'
should be associated with those who actively develop the quality of their
students' learning, rather than those pushing forward the frontiers ever
so slightly in some tiny area of subject specialism. It is increasingly argued
(Ramsden, 1992) that however competent higher education teachers

may be in their subject area, they need to aspire to being distinguished teachers as well. Perhaps the most productive way towards such a position is to encourage teachers to become competent educational researchers, and help them to ensure that their research is recognized and valued.

CAN WE IDENTIFY RESEARCH COMPETENCES?

In many disciplines, NVQ competence-based frameworks have already been drawn up, attempting in their own way to identify and explain the competences which are intended to be developed in training programmes, and the evidence which should be brought forward to claim accreditation for such competences. Can we look forward to a NVQ framework describing competences relating to research? If we are to try to produce a blueprint for such a framework, it will mean working out the details of three parameters along the following lines:

- statements of the relevant competences ('can do' statements? – or are they merely 'has done' statements, or worse, 'did do once' statements?);

- performance criteria showing exactly how the competences should be demonstrated;

- range statements showing the conditions under which the competences should be demonstrated, and giving further details of the evidence which will indicate successful demonstration of the competences;

- 'grading criteria' in selected theme areas, helping performances to be classified as 'pass', 'merit' and 'distinction'.

Or is research something quite special, something beyond the scope of competence descriptors and evidence specifications? It may be tempting to say one or more of the following of research:

- you know good research when you see it;

- if you can *measure* it, it isn't it;

- it's much more complex than can be adequately described by mechanistic frameworks.

Several 'research competence' agendas

In one way or another, attempts have been made to judge research competence for many years. Whenever an application for funding of a research proposal is considered, and whenever a proposal for a new research studentship is drawn up, those processing the applications apply performance criteria of one sort or another to the evidence laid before them. One such criterion is bound to be along the lines of 'has already delivered high quality research'. However, even that criterion is likely to be inextricably linked with evidence, and probably also with 'range statements' of a form. But what is 'successful research'? There are several overlapping possibilities:

- research where the aims and objectives have been demonstrably achieved, and where there are tangible outcomes that are useful in the field;

- research as above, but where the products of the research are successfully published and made available to other workers in the field, and where critical review by peers substantiates the validity and reliability of the research;

- research which adds to the field of human knowledge, for example by reporting new information or explaining things which have not been explained before;

- research which builds on existing knowledge, and makes possible new applications and new developments.

THE RELATIONSHIPS BETWEEN TEACHING AND RESEARCH

In higher education, many – or most – new lecturers are appointed largely on the basis of their expertise in their subject disciplines. A major contributing factor may be their records of research publications in their fields. At more senior levels, subject-related expertise is seen as even more important. When it comes to applying for promotion, or for senior appointments at another institution, a track record of successful research publications is a vital component of the sort of *curriculum vitae* that gets one onto interview shortlists.

It is often said that involvement in current state-of-the-art research is a valuable contributory factor towards good teaching. After all, someone who spends at least some time pushing back the frontiers of knowledge and understanding in a discipline will be a formative influence on the next generation of people who will carry on the good work. Or could this be looked on rather less kindly as a view whereby the main product of good teaching should be to engender the skills and attitudes needed by future researchers? How many of our students will make their careers out of research? (I recently advertised for a research assistant; the advertisement attracted some 121 applications from a wide range of hopeful candidates. My sympathies go to the 120 who were unsuccessful.)

It can, however, be argued that the most effective teachers *are* researchers, but not usually in the conventional sense. Effective teachers are usually researchers into teaching and learning processes. They are usually skilled observers of such processes. They are often experimenters, trying out new techniques and ideas. They seek feedback proactively to give themselves data on which to base new approaches and experiments. Sadly perhaps, such researching teachers may often not play that vital part of the research game – being seen to have researched successfully.

Despite the amount of published educational research, there are many excellent innovators and discoverers whose work is known only to those students whose learning experiences are enhanced by the effects of the research effort going into the teaching they encounter. Furthermore, even when researching teachers successfully publish their work in the educational literature, there are always those who say, 'Well, under what *subject* exactly can we classify these publications; is it endocrinology, or research into *teaching* endocrinology, or research into how people *learn* about endocrinology?'

A FUNDAMENTAL RESEARCH AGENDA

Research of any kind is essentially the systematic and informed search for the answers to a mere six basic questions, and making sense of data gathered to explain the findings to other people. The most useful questions are usually the most basic – those that have underpinned the quest for human knowledge since the dawn of recorded history:

- Why? (Why should I learn this? Why is it important?)

- What? (What exactly should I learn? What is the value? What should I do with it?)

- Who? (Who has already researched the subject and what did they find?)

- Where? (Where will I seek further information and data?)

- When? (When do I need to apply the results of my learning? When is it most relevant?)

- How? (How can I explain it? How can I made sense of it all? How can I use it? How can I extend it?)

RESEARCH METHODOLOGY

There are numerous courses in 'research methods'. Students undertaking Masters programmes may be required to follow such courses. PhD
students may be encouraged to participate, or even required to attend.
But what are the basic ingredients of the methodology of successful
research? Most such 'menus' I have seen seem to be a rather arbitrary
mixture of bits from other disciplines. 'Statistics' always features somewhere, yet how often do we see scientific statistical analysis techniques
applied wildly beyond the scope where they may be valid or useful? While
it is possible to compute standard deviations from quite small data
samples, I've seen such techniques used blindly to deliver impressive-
looking figures which turn out to be based on raw data which are so
unreliable when we get down to looking carefully at them, as to be
statistically quite meaningless. For example, where people make decisions on a Likert-scale relating to two contrasting statements, sometimes
the statements themselves are so complex that they can have several
different 'meanings' to different readers, depending which sub-clauses
happened to linger in the mind while making the decision. Sometimes
the statements are far from being opposite ends of a scale, but instead
overlap in a complex way. And yet, because the science of statistics can
deliver numerical parameters from data (however flawed the data may
be), the numerical parameters seem to be taken seriously by the majority
of editors and journal referees, and the research is subsequently published.

However, if research methodology can be 'taught', it should be possible to identify the intended outcomes of such courses, and in turn it
should be possible to describe the outcomes in terms of the competences
which researchers should be able to demonstrate. It should also be possible to illustrate the kinds of evidence which would be acceptable
demonstrations of their achievement of the outcomes. In fact, perhaps if
the intended outcomes of such courses were expressed really clearly,
there may be no need to have research methodology courses as such, but
instead simply to require researchers to develop their evidence of their
own competences to demonstrate that their methodology was sound and
reliable.

CREATIVE THINKING, PROBLEM SOLVING, PLANNING AND STRATEGY

All of these are 'in' words and phrases in thinking about successful
research. But can these things be 'taught'? Especially when it comes to

strategy and planning, perhaps the most important ingredient in a portfolio of skills for successful research is *flexibility*. Successful researchers learn from their mistakes. A plan which works out well right from the outset is probably too simple. The real advances are often made when a plan does not work as expected, leading to critical reflection and further creativity in the search for new approaches to a situation. In most areas of life, learning from mistakes is a reality. In research, this is bound to be so also. Yet discussions of research planning and strategy tend to shy away from the possibility (let alone probability) of 'getting it wrong' at first. In my own discipline-specific research early in my career, I well remember spending weeks working out by trial and error how to make some experimental measurements, then making the 'real' measurements *and* writing the research paper in a single afternoon.

RESEARCH AND LEARNING PROCESSES

In several recent publications, I have advocated a down-to-earth model of learning processes based on the answers that thousands of people have given me to simple questions about their own learning experiences. In short, the four factors which are important contributors towards successful learning appear to be as follows:

- *wanting to learn* – motivation, sense of purpose, clear intentions;
- *learning by doing* – practice, learning from mistakes, learning from experience;
- *feedback* – peer review, seeing the results, measuring the successes and failures;
- *digesting* – making sense of the learning experience, making sense of the feedback.

Perhaps these four dimensions of successful learning are equally important as dimensions of successful research. Perhaps research methodology programmes could usefully address each of these four processes, and assist researchers to develop coherent approaches to research by treating research as any normal learning process and not as a specialized phenomenon to be indulged in a completely different way than the rest of human progress. Moreover, I believe that all four stages are necessarily involved in any successful research work which in due course manifests itself in the form accepted as evidence of high-quality research – in other words as reputable publications. Perhaps a preliminary breakdown of the 'wanting, doing, feedback, digesting' model of learning into research-related competences and attitudes may be as follows:

Wanting

- the motivation which keeps successful PhD students going;
- the intention to plan the research work effectively;
- the intention to learn from doing, and from mistakes as well as from triumphs;
- the intention to seek feedback from every available source;
- the intention to use feedback constructively, whether the feedback be positive or critical;
- the intention to make sense of the learning experiences, and to communicate the findings in a coherent and meaningful way to other workers in the field.

Doing

- developing and applying competence in 'research methodology' areas;
- trying a range of approaches to 'doing' so that the approaches which deliver the most useful results can be identified and fostered;
- selecting the 'research methodology' tools and devices which are meaningful and relevant in the context of the research;
- keeping track of the processes of the research as a documented learning experience, so that greater skill at designing processes for future research work will develop;
- learning from and accepting 'failures' as a productive part of learning-by-doing.

Feedback

- continuously seeking feedback on the success (or otherwise) of the choice of research processes;
- continuously using feedback on the validity and reliability of research findings;
- continuously responding to feedback in the design of adjustments and refinements in research methodology;

- seeking feedback on the appropriateness (or otherwise) of the application of statistical methods to the data accumulated.

Digesting

- making sense of the findings of the research, in an analytical and objective manner;

- additionally, making sense of the research findings in appropriate speculative and creative ways (giving due acknowledgement to the differences between proof, deduction, speculation and imagination);

- accepting and acknowledging the status of subjective views and opinions, and presenting these to complement (but not interfere with) objective analysis and deduction;

- communicating the products of the research and analysis, in ways which are understood clearly by fellow-researchers in the field;

- communicating the essence of the products of the research and analysis in ways which can be understood by practitioners in the field;

- communicating the essence of the product of the research and analysis in ways which will help new learners in the field to gain an appreciation of the main issues, questions, and conclusions.

In many ways, research is as natural a part of 'being human' as is learning in its broadest sense. It is important, then, to accept that the competences which underpin effective research are not in fact completely separate from those competences which have enabled the human species to develop and advance. We do not need to sit down at our 'research desks' and try to switch on a completely different set of thinking processes or communication skills from those which we use in our day-to-day work – or indeed our survival as human beings. It is the same brain that organizes our daily lives that we will apply to the task of structuring our researches and communicating our findings.

More importantly, any dedicated teacher will want to know more about how students' learning is going, and about how teaching approaches can help students to learn even more effectively and successfully. Educational research, to a dedicated teacher, is as natural as wishing to improve any other 'performance' in our day-to-day lives. Perhaps the time is right to put all of this educational research firmly on the 'research table', and justify it alongside all the other kinds of research which 'count' so much.

WHAT IS 'RESEARCH WHICH COUNTS'?

Recent events in the UK have polarized research (educational research included) into 'research which counts', and research which isn't taken very seriously by those responsible for deciding which is 'high-quality' research. There are unofficial 'lists' of acceptable journals and 'also-rans'. With the emphasis on peer-reviewed publication, there is already a spate of new journals and new specialisms. Practitioners who happen to have written best-selling textbooks for students are probably disadvantaged when compared to researchers who have written specialist research publications in a few elite journals, and whose work is studied only by a handful of fellow-specialists. If research methodology competences are to be taken seriously, surely those competences which relate to 'being seen to have succeeded by those whose opinion counts' need to be identified, fostered and developed? Or perhaps it is the case that the rules of the game need to be changed. At present, for example, in many research journals, one of the quality criteria knowingly or subconsciously taken into account when deciding whether to publish a new contribution to the field is 'reference to the existing literature' in the field. In this situation, researchers naturally develop the skill of smattering their writing with passages along the following lines:

'It has already been stated (Smith and Jones, 1989) that there are at least five advantages of including research methodology courses in taught Masters degree programmes. Indeed, we have already added some of our own views to the debate (Myself and Partner, 1990, 1991a, 1991b, 1992, 1994, 1995 [in press]). Despite the concerns raised (eg, Barker and Corbett, 1990) that such courses may not address fundamental issues, it has been accepted (Arbuthnott, 1991) that such courses should nonetheless be provided in the hope that during them, new researchers may adjust their approaches towards the meta-cognitive psychodominant behaviour appropriate to the development of creative socioeconomic pseudo-synthetic abilities said to be necessary for the creation of new ways of communicating ideas to the world of business, industry and commerce, as well as to the members of the Editorial Board of the foremost journal in the field (ibid) (see also Todhunter-Brown, 1992). The present work, however, advocates that...

Reading the research literature in many disciplines is not as far removed from the above scenario as may be desired! Moreover, the contributions which dedicated teaching professionals are able to add to the research literature are certain to be far more interesting and relevant than the sort of work lampooned above. It is in a quest for the best ways forward for educational research that the remainder of this chapter will search for some ways of pinning down the best elements of 'research competence'.

A DRAFT FRAMEWORK OF RESEARCH COMPETENCE

In the light of the above discussion, this chapter concludes with the following (real, imaginary and purely provocative) framework for the sort of competence which may (or should) underpin the realization of meaningful research. The four categories of research mentioned at the outset of this chapter are addressed in turn, namely, competences relating to:

- research methodology;

- successful publication of research findings;

- successful research into teaching and learning processes and practices;

- successfully turning the outcomes of good teaching
  developments into 'the right kinds' of published research.

Each competence is expressed in a broad 'can do' statement, some performance indicators, and some suggestions along the lines of 'evidence descriptors' or 'grading criteria' on the basis of which 'high-quality' research may be distinguished from all the other material which presently fills up thousands of pages in hundreds of research journals!

However, is this the right approach?

Now, with NVQ frameworks and GNVQ specifications, syllabus content is progressively being expressed in terms of what learners will become able to demonstrate (competence elements and performance criteria), details of the circumstances in which they will be able to demonstrate their performance (range descriptors) and further details of the sort of evidence they will be required to furnish to demonstrate their competences (evidence indicators). However detailed these specifications are, they usually avoid (or indeed take great care to avoid) addressing whether or not learners *understand* what they have learned.

Let us take a critical look at any typical 'Unit of Competence 013' (people seem to like giving these things reference numbers). Imagine now a detailed NVQ-type specification for educational research. I've included in my imaginary specification a number of phrases which are all-too-common in real NVQ specifications and referred to these phrases in the comments to follow. My comments might be:

At first sight a typical unit of competence in educational research seems to be very helpful – seven (say) performance criteria are listed,

details are given about the 'range', and the underpinning knowledge. Even better, perhaps, guidance is given to assessors (this
should be of value to learners too). Finally, 'sources of evidence' are
specified.

The 'headings' are fine! It's the words which are under the headings
that are (in my opinion) far from satisfactory. For example, a phrase
such as 'information is drawn from appropriate sources' is not very
helpful as a performance criterion for the simple reason that it is
supposed that there is some automatic ability (on the part of tutors,
trainers, learners and assessors) to agree on the meaning of the
adjective 'appropriate'. Phrases such as 'Information is verified,
interpreted and summarized accurately' seem laudable, but again
there is no guidance regarding *what sort* of information is really
intended to be handled. In other words, the knowledge and
understanding dimensions are missing from the specification of
intended competence. The creative, developmental and strategic
dimensions are not just missing but entirely unable to be related to
the terminology of the specification.

'Information is prepared for relevant alternative policies and
plans'; again this seems a praiseworthy performance criterion, but
the word 'relevant' helps neither trainers, learners nor assessors.
What exactly is intended, I ask? How would it be decided that
information may be *irrelevant?*

Need I go further? All these performance criteria are sensible, but
far too vague to define the sorts of performance that are to be
sought. It can be argued – and I have a lot of sympathy with the
argument – that attempts to reduce such skills as 'research' into
competence terms tend to lead to definitions of *minimum* competence rather than targets for significant development.

'Guidance for assessors' is a helpful heading – but look at how
unhelpful the guidance actually is. 'All performance criteria must be
met' – surely this is obvious? 'Minimum number of successful
assessment occasions: 3' – what on earth does this mean? Perhaps if
this criterion were applied to the driving test, our roads would be
safer places to travel. But what is an 'assessment occasion'? Even
worse, there follows the statement that 'all variables within the range
statement must be assessed on at least one occasion'. Alright,
everything important should be assessed at least once – but look back
at that 'Range statement': 'Requirements: statutory, non-statutory',
for example. So what exactly is it that should be assessed? This
competence-based description does little to help.

After this digression into how trivializing it can be to apply formalistic frameworks to the definition of complex competences, I hope you may agree that it would be much better if research competences could be linked to the 'wanting, doing, feedback and digesting' stages of the processes of learning and research. To end this chapter, however, I would like to try to apply a structured framework to some of the competences which may connect research and teaching, but I stress that this is only a start – and not a good one!

1. A sample competence relating to research methodology

Can do: *keep abreast with research in my specialist area.*
Performance indicators:

● *review relevant journals and periodicals at least twice per month*

● *keep a card-file system (or computer database) of relevant articles*

● *attend at least one specialist conference each year*

● *give a paper at a conference at least once every two years.*

Evidence descriptors:

● *up-to-date card index showing current references and comments*

● *records taken at subject-conferences in the last two years*

● *paper to be presented at a conference later this year.*

Grading criteria:

Pass: *adequate evidence of keeping track with current research*
Merit: *good up-to-date records of new articles, thorough reviews and notes of conferences attended*
Distinction: *very detailed analysis of new contributions to the literature in the field; at least one major new contribution presented at a conference in the last two years.*

Note: but this is just a basic competence – perhaps one we take for granted in research. Is it adequately expressed here? I doubt it.

2. A sample competence relating to successful publication of research findings

Can do: *publish articles in the 'right' journals to count in the next Research Assessment Exercise.*

Performance indicators:

- *finds out which are the 'right' Journals.*

- *makes friends with members of the Editorial Boards of these journals.*

- *gets three articles published in time for the research assessment exercise.*

Evidence descriptors:

- *Three (or more) articles published in the 'right' journals.*

Grading criteria:

Pass: *two articles in reasonable journals*
Merit: *three articles in quite reputable journals*
Distinction: *four or more articles in really reputable journals.*

3. A sample competence relating to successful research into teaching and learning in particular
(This time I will try to be serious!)

Can do: *make significant advances in good practice in the context of teaching and learning in the subject discipline involved.*
Performance indicators:

- *has analysed the principal problems faced by learners in tackling the subject*

- *has devised solutions to these problems, and tested them out with learners involved in the discipline*

- *has gathered feedback from learners, and analysed the effectiveness of the improvements to their learning experiences.*

Evidence descriptors:

- *a published analysis of the problems learners have with the discipline*

- *a published account of solutions to learners' problems, and their feedback on the new approaches used to solve them.*

Grading criteria:

Pass: *work published in 'New Academic'*
Merit: *work published as a SEDA Paper*
Distinction: *work published by McGraw-Hill*

(sorry, couldn't be serious for long enough!)

4. Competences relating to producing successful research publications relating to teaching and learning?

(As you will have seen, I've already included this dimension under the 'Grading criteria' for '3' above! Perhaps this shows how indistinguishable the categories really are.)

CONCLUSIONS

The theme of this chapter provided an interesting workshop for many participants at the November 1994 SEDA Conference held at Dyffryn House, near Cardiff. However, despite trying hard, we did not manage to come up with a convincing framework of the research competences (and in particular, educational development competences) which should be looked for in the advancement of our field. We did, however, come up with some serious reservations regarding how research has been 'assessed' in the past, and how people will at present be 'adjusting the products of their research' to gain them maximum credit in the next round of research assessment. We still feel, sadly, that research into the teaching and learning of subjects is still quite out in the cold (as far as being recognized as being important is concerned), yet we are convinced that research into teaching and learning of individual subjects is ultimately of far more worth than simply subject-specific research. Our destiny is in the hands of our today's learners – never forget that.

REFERENCE

Ramsden, P (1992) *Learning to Teach in Higher Education*, London:Routledge.

Chapter 9

A Broader Education for Research Students: Changing the Culture

Lin Thorley and Roy Gregory

INTRODUCTION

The education of a research student in the United Kingdom has echoes of an apprenticeship system. At its worst this can mean that the student is at the mercy of an idiosyncratic relationship with a supervisor and a narrow initiation into a discipline mind-set and world view. The focus is on a narrow topic area, with many pressures to conform to the discipline paradigm.

Many students fall by the wayside in this process. Others who succeed receive a narrow education which we believe is not best suited to our complex modern society. Even successful students often experience frustration and isolation. Research education easily becomes a retreat into a safer individualized world without the personal development challenges of operating in multi-disciplinary teams and dealing with complex personal and social issues. The supervisor/student relationship often remains unchallenged and is vulnerable to misuse and abuse.

In response to national and university concerns about research training, including those of the type expressed above, a research methodology course has now been introduced at the University of Hertfordshire. The intention was to improve the process of acquiring the skills and to accelerate learning the practice of research, increase completion rates for research degrees and give students a broader-based learning experience. However, the university was unsure how these things might best be done and approached us to help in designing a course.

Our fundamental decision was to take a personal development approach rather than simply offer skills input. We already had considerable experience in working with undergraduates and academics in the areas of personal skills (Gregory, 1993; Thorley, 1992), personal development, group-work and improving teaching and learning (Gregory and Thorley, 1993). But we had little previous experience working with research students and none concerning this particular type of course.

We decided to begin by running a pilot residential course, which would involve the students at an early stage and establish a process of continuous reflection, evaluation and improvement as the course was delivered. The main aims of the residential were to encourage autonomous learning and self-development, including personal and skills development and to increase support for students' studies using experiential learning methods and 'action learning'-type groups (McGill and Beaty 1992).

DESCRIPTION OF COURSE

From this beginning a full research methodology course has now been developed, equivalent to two modules. It consists of three parts:

● an Induction Programme (half module);

● the Personal Development of the Researcher – practice (one module); and

● Research 'Tools' and Techniques sessions – theory appropriate in a cross-discipline setting (half module).

Some discipline areas also expect their students to attend extra sessions particular to their subject specification.

The course was approved by the Research Degrees Committee of the university in July 1993. It is now a compulsory part of the programme for all full-time research students and must be passed before students can transfer from an MPhil to a PhD programme. It is strongly encouraged, though cannot easily be enforced, for part-timers. The course fulfils new national requirements for research student training.

While we have been involved in developing the whole course, the aspect we are most concerned with here is the personal development module, based on the two-day residential. This has now run twice, with about 20 students on each course. It focuses on the idea of personal development as a continuous process, on working as a cross-disciplinary group and on active use of the experiential learning cycle.

The learning groups of five or six members meet twice during the residential itself and are required to meet at least three times more when back in college. A short reflective learning log is written during and after the residential and a longer second one is kept throughout the student's first year. This second log is based on the student's experience of their own development in relation to the research process. Students are encouraged to record their thoughts on each stage of the learning cycle, as well as feelings and other learning insights as they develop as a researcher.

Skills development is undertaken on an individual basis by identifying the specific aspects of the experiential learning cycle and learning to use them in a planned and conscious way. Further help is given in this area by the use of a personal skills development pack (Thorley, 1992) and by the availability of literature and video material on personal skills. During the residential the group generates its own list of the personal skills they most want to develop as a 'menu' of skills sessions to be arranged by us and offered over the next few months.

Assessment covers the whole course and is on a pass or fail basis. It is based on attendance, active participation, a presentation given at an internal research seminar, and the two reflective learning logs.

COURSE DEVELOPMENTAL PROCESS

The residentials and subsequent skills sessions run so far have been evaluated by questionnaire and discussion and the feedback used in designing the final approved course. There was general support among students and most supervisors for a course designed to meet the needs of research students. There were, however, a wide variety of views from students and supervisors concerning the usefulness of the 'content' of the residential courses. There was a strong tendency in evaluation responses to focus on 'content', with little appreciation of the importance of understanding or of the 'process' of learning and development.

Many of the students arrived at the first residential with negative attitudes related to the way they felt they were being treated as research students. Some resented the 'time out' or had isolationist attitudes. It was clear that they did not understand the possible benefits of such a course. Unfortunately these attitudes were shared and in some cases fostered by supervisors. Some, mostly students on their own in a research area, came with a sense of relief that they would at last meet other researchers. For them the course was a great success. However, the first residential in particular needed all our skills simply to 'turn round' the atmosphere to something positive. By the end we felt we had succeeded in doing so.

During the course a significant number of students expressed real resistance to the idea that mixed-discipline learning groups could help them to discuss their research with others outside their own subject and that they could learn from such groups. They also found it difficult at a time of intense work within their discipline area to step outside their own paradigms and see the need for personal development. It became clear that the course was challenging some of the basic assumptions of research education for both supervisors and students. A significant cultural shift was required to gain acceptance of the value of what was seen by some as 'additional work' and a distraction from the 'real programme of study'. Research students generally appear to acquire considerable critical skills directed outwards but little in the way of self-critical skills to direct at their personal areas or at their own discipline-based assumptions (as opposed to discipline-content). There was a general and noticeable lack of 'self-awareness' which was difficult to address and yet vital to self-development.

We began to realize that while the research apprenticeship system inducts students into a discipline-specific paradigm that turns them into 'real' chemists, engineers and so on, almost by narrowing them down and task-centring them, we were suggesting a developmental broadening out, and a process-centred model. The two approaches were in fundamental opposition.

After a number of meetings of the learning groups there was a generally more positive attitude towards them. There seemed to be a growing view among the students that the groups could be of considerable benefit in providing a place for relationships to develop and for personal issues to be discussed. The groups have tended, however, not to fulfil their full 'action learning' potential and there is a need for much better preparation in future residential courses.

The assessment issue proved difficult and had to be discussed with the students on numerous occasions. They needed clarification of the criteria and also the way the reflective learning logs would be assessed. This type of work, which requires a good deal of personal involvement with the subject, was new to many of the students who were predominantly science/technology based. Many students found the reflective activity difficult in itself and consequently found it hard to write the learning logs. Their difficulty with the assessment system seemed to reflect their difficulty with the course in general, and it was noticeable that there was a good deal of mistrust to begin with.

The second residential course was shortened from three to two days to remove some of the frustrations of 'time out' from research expressed by students. More concentration was put on the skills of presentation and the students were put into learning groups earlier to give a better focus for the course. An exercise on reflection was included in the programme but students still found this and the logs difficult. We also put more emphasis in the second course on explaining the reasons behind the 'learning process' rather than 'skills content' approach. The group was more diverse than the first, but again there was a mixed reaction and the same tendency for some students to take a narrow view of research education. There was still a lack of appreciation among many students that personal development would be of benefit to them both immediately in their research and in their future careers. Others, though, were very positive about the experience.

CONTINUING DEVELOPMENT

During the 1993–4 session we expect to run three further residentials. The introduction of personal and skills development through experiential learning, the motivation of students to broadening their education and more effective use of learning groups are still major challenges for improvement.

We intend to address the need for researchers to undertake self-development more directly next time. Wherever possible we will enhance the perceived relevance of the course by linking self- and skills development to what will occur as part of the research programme. We will also address the conflict identified earlier between a narrow subject focus often encouraged by the research project and supervisor, and a broader outlook and ability to learn from outside the discipline.

OTHER BENEFITS OF THE COURSE

There have been a number of positive spin-offs from the course in addition to the intended outcomes. Student feedback raised issues at university level that have now been addressed. Thus the student registration and induction process has been improved, a university research tutor appointed, training seminars organized for supervisors and the Postgraduate Student Society re-started.

Students from the residential course contributed to the supervisor training sessions, discussing issues of good and bad practice in supervision. These sessions were particularly powerful in producing change. Individual supervisors can have very different perceptions of their role and these perceptions are not necessarily shared with their students. There were examples quoted of very different degrees of control and support given in supervision. Students often have to guess their tutors' assumptions as to how to proceed in the relationship. They seem to feel surprisingly powerless if problems arise. There is still much to be done in changing attitudes and spreading good practice if standards of supervision are to be improved. Involving students in this process is crucial.

CONCLUDING REMARKS

For us, developing the course has involved a steep learning curve. We initially underestimated the extent of the cultural change required. Much has now been achieved at university level and in raising awareness amongst individual supervisors and students. Students are now better prepared for their work and the standard of supervision has become an important quality issue. There are still, however, many to convince and many improvements to be made.

The course development process used has proved to be successful and has enabled the course to be running and approved within a relatively short time. The residential element provides an important focus for the research students and for the whole course. It allows a period of intensive focusing on self-development and experiential learning in a way that is perceived to be relevant and useful by the majority of research students. The use of learning groups and reflective learning logs has been difficult and met with only partial success so far. Both need working on.

There remains a need for resolution of the perceived conflict by some supervisors and students between their research work and a broader-based postgraduate education. It is hoped that on-going discussion and training of supervisors will help to inculcate a broader approach, and that ways will be found to bridge the short-term aims and goals of supervisors and students and the long-term needs of a broader-based research education.

REFERENCES

Gregory, R (1993) *Student Self-Appraisal Pack*, University of Hertfordshire.

Gregory, R and Thorley, L (1993) 'Deep and surface approaches to learning to teach engineering', Proceedings of the SEFI International Conference, Lulea, Sweden.

McGill, I and Beaty, L (1992) *Action Learning: A practitioners guide*, London: Kogan Page.

Thorley, L (1992) *Develop Your Personal Skills: A do-it-yourself pack for students*, Hatfield: University of Hertfordshire.

Chapter 10

A Staff Development Programme for Supervisors of Research Students

Ivan Moore

INTRODUCTION

Research degree students are facing increasing pressures to complete their theses in ever shorter times; additionally, new forms of doctorate are being introduced which will require the development of new skills for supervisors. Results of the recent Research Assessment Exercise (RAE) have encouraged universities to increase their output in terms of successful DPhils. With these developments in mind, the research degrees sub-committee at the University of Ulster approached Staff Development with a request for the department to provide some form of staff development for research student supervisors.

This chapter discusses the Staff Development response and outlines the development methodology of the academic staff development officer. It shows how training needs were identified and prioritized, how staff were identified and recruited and how the course was designed. A programme for the first phase is included.

A STATEMENT OF THE PROBLEM

The Research Degrees Subcommittee of the University of Ulster approached Staff Development in April 1993. The committee identified several challenges facing research degree students and invited Staff Development to advise them on a suitable programme which would help the university meet these challenges. After discussion with the chair of the committee, the main pressures facing students were identified as:

- *Externally imposed grant sanctions* – units of assessment which did not meet a 40 per cent submission target on a three-year rolling average were to be sanctioned by the Department of Education for Northern

Ireland (DENI). These sanctions would remove the quota awards and would be imposed for up to three years.

- *Pressure to improve completion rates* – the 40 per cent completion rate was to be raised to 60 per cent by DENI. This would put many units which had escaped sanctions under an increased pressure.

- *A reduction in submission times* – the university had decided to reduce the submission rate from four years to three.

- *The Research Assessment Exercise* – this assessment had produced better than expected grades for some units of assessment which had not been viewed as major research units by the university and which had no previous experience of research degree student programmes. These units were now being encouraged to formulate a DPhil programme.

ANALYSIS OF THE TRAINING NEEDS

Consultation with the committee and with other experienced researchers and coordinators of units of assessment identified good supervision of the students by staff as a crucial success factor in meeting these demands. Further, three areas were identified as benefiting from investment in training provision for supervisors:

- An *'induction' programme for inexperienced supervisors* – many staff in the university are actively involved in research but have never supervised a DPhil student before. Such staff wishing to do so are required to act as a second supervisor before the university will recognize them as competent to become first supervisors. An extensive training programme for these staff would enable them to gain approval more quickly and it would ensure that good practice was disseminated to these staff rather than the current system which relied on the (untested) expertise of the first supervisor, both as a supervisor and as a good mentor to the novice supervisor.

- *Development courses* – these courses would be aimed at experienced supervisors and would tackle issues such as achieving three-year submission rates, supervising part-time students, different forms of doctorate and their role as external examiners.

- *Targeted courses* – these courses would be aimed at two groups of supervisors:
  - units of assessment which had, *as a unit*, no experience of supervising DPhil students;

–   Units of assessment which had been sanctioned.
The training needs and approaches of these two units would be different.

PRIORITIZING THE TRAINING NEEDS

A working group consisting of both expert and novice supervisors was drawn together to develop the training programmes.

As a first stage, the group identified the priorities as:

● Induction

● Targeted development

DEVELOPING THE INDUCTION PROGRAMME

Three approaches were considered:

● to purchase the expertise of a recognized training provider in this field;

● to deliver the programme in-house, using internal expertise;

● to use both in-house and external expertise.

A planning team was convened to consider the shape of the programme. At its first meeting in October, the team used a range of active techniques to determine the main characteristics of a good supervisor and of a successful DPhil programme. Using these techniques, the team identified models of good practice in the area and conditions which were most likely to lead to successful completion of a DPhil. The outcomes of this planning session were summarized and used to produce a model of good supervision practice for use in the workshop:

The workshop would follow the principles of active learning (group work, case studies, role plays etc).

● it was decided that an external facilitator should be used;

● the facilitator would be given a very specific brief;

● internal staff would also be used as leaders/facilitators;

● the workshop would require three days, and would be residential;

- the workshop would cater for 25 participants;
- a blend of participants would be sought from across all units of assessment.

Content

The group identified eight areas for consideration in the workshop:

Background

- national, local and internal developments in DPhils;
- the importance of doctorate programmes;
- University procedures.

Supervisor-student relationship

- the formal and the informal;
- what if things go wrong?

The product

- what is a doctorate?
- the end product.

Generic skills

- oral and written communication;
- presenting papers;
- teamwork.

Admission

- a 'good' student;
- a 'good' topic.

A good environment

- full- and part-time students.

Managing the research

- getting started;
- milestones;
- monitoring;
- records;
- project management;
- upgrading/transfer.

UU procedures

- critical analysis;
- a charter for postgraduate students.

An external provider was identified and the programme was validated at the national SEDA conference on Research and Teaching in Higher Education, in Cardiff during November 1993.

Refining the programme

Feedback from the conference and from the external provider was considered by the planning team. The main development to the programme arose from a recognition that, since the course participants were not experienced supervisors, it would be necessary to be more directive than at first envisaged. Additionally, it was felt important to ensure that any useful conclusions, good practices or ideas or suggestions for improvement of unit or university procedures and practices would be fed back effectively to the units of assessment. Therefore a *second agenda* was developed by carefully selecting the internal group facilitators from the various units. Staff were identified on the basis of their credibility within their unit, so that their feedback to their units would be well received.

In addition to this, an interview with the vice-chancellor identified the importance of ensuring that we do not 'train dinosaurs', as he put it. New forms of doctorate are being developed within the university and this group of generally fairly recently appointed or qualified staff would be the most likely group to develop these new programmes. It was therefore decided to strengthen this aspect of the workshops.

The Final Programme

Components of the final programme included:

- managing research – good practice
- introductory skills for students
- compulsory courses
- links to theses
- M Phil/D Phil upgrade
- admission/assessing potential
- generic skills of communication, written and oral skills, presenting papers and teamwork
- the supervisor/student relationship
- clarifying the nature of doctorate
- monitoring progress criteria for success
- preparing for a *viva*
- assessment: exploring a PhD
- university procedures : a charter for students.

100 Research, Teaching and Learning in HE

An interesting feature of the final programme was the 'any questions' session at which course participants will be able to gain insights into the university's view of its doctorate programme as well as clarifying any points or issues raised during the early sessions of the course. The panel will include the vice-chancellor, the pro-vice-chancellor for planning and research and the head of the research office. It will be chaired by one of the deans.

It is anticipated that the final session 'University procedures' will provide useful ideas for feedback to the units of assessment.

IDENTIFYING THE COURSE PARTICIPANTS

The planning team decided that the most appropriate method of identifying course participants was through the coordinators of the units of assessment. A letter was sent to these coordinators along with a form on which they identified and prioritized those staff who would fit the criteria for selection. It was felt that this method would allow the university to identify those staff who would benefit most from the programme and from whom the university would obtain the best return for the investment. After the first course has been delivered, the workshop will be advertised to all academic staff and research officers so that all staff will have the opportunity to benefit from the programme.

There are 24 units of assessment in the university, and the response from the coordinators was so positive that it is likely that the workshop will have to be delivered six or seven times to satisfy the need. Thereafter, the course will be delivered when sufficient 'new' staff have been recruited to make the course viable.

The first course was delivered in January 1994 and the participants were invited from across the units of assessment (one from each unit, prioritized by the coordinator).

It is interesting to note here that some units have identified so many candidates that it will be possible to organize a special workshop for those units.

CONCLUSION

The programme was developed by Staff Development in response to a need identified by the institution. Staff Development has managed the needs identification, planning, recruitment, administration and delivery of the programme and is meeting the costs. It is anticipated that the programme will be delivered several times over the next two years and that it will interlace with the other training areas which were identified by the panel.

Staff Development, the planning team and the university are confident that this major programme will ensure improvement in our DPhil programme through the continuing professional development of research degree student supervisors. They are also confident that the programme will help the university to introduce new forms of doctorate programmes and to carry them through to a successful conclusion.

Chapter 11

Research-related Staff Development
– An Approach

Irene Harris

INTRODUCTION

With the change to university status has come an increased emphasis on the role of research and the expectation that most academic staff will engage in research activity. Consequently a number of research-related staff development initiatives have been introduced at institutional, faculty and departmental levels. This chapter details developments, in one faculty, at the Manchester Metropolitan University.

For many staff this emphasis on research represents a significant change. In the Faculty of Management and Business, as elsewhere in the old polytechnic sector, staff were often recruited for their business-related skills and knowledge. The need to recognize and cater for the different starting points of staff was therefore an important influence on this initiative. From the outset our aims regarding this staff development initiative were to:

- stimulate debate;

- dispel some 'myths';

- involve staff in identifying their own development needs;

- encourage staff to 'share' skills and knowledge;

- provide a supportive environment for staff new to research.

The main methods adopted which are described in this chapter were:

- faculty seminars – designed to cater for a wide audience

- a Research Skills course of three hours a week for eight weeks

- specific development activities to meet staff demands;

- departmental research seminar series;
- faculty doctoral programme.

So far the developments have been well received by staff and demand is high for more workshops/seminars/courses. Although it is too early to fully review this initiative we feel that our initial experience highlights a number of issues which may be of wider interest to staff developers and others with a remit to stimulate research activity.

CONSIDERING THE BROADER CONTEXT

Emphasis on change is all around these days – it is difficult to pick up a journal or newspaper without reference to the changes in organizations and the consequent changes required of staff. Terms such as, 'lifelong learning', 'continuous development' and 'multiskilling' are a familiar part of the language of change. Higher education is no exception. Changes abound throughout the sector including:

- rising student numbers and non-traditional entry;
- reduced unit funding;
- emphasis on developing employment-related skills;
- end of the binary divide;
- quality assessment and audit.

All of these changes, and others, impact on the role of the academic.

One aspect of ending the binary divide in the 'new' universities has been the increased emphasis on research and scholarly activity. At the same time institutions have been required to introduce personal performance reviews for academic staff. So, the institutional change of emphasis, towards research, has been clearly reinforced at a personal level. Many staff in the polytechnic sector regarded teaching as their highest priority and did not have a background, or indeed an interest, in research. The emphasis on involvement in research has thus represented a significant change for many staff.

INSTITUTIONAL CONTEXT

The faculty of Management and Business at the Manchester Metropolitan University has over 150 full-time academic staff, in five departments, and more than 4,000 students, (full- and part-time). In the 1992/3 HEFCE research selectivity exercise the faculty gained a 2 rating. In its overall strategic plan the faculty is committed to raising its research profile in terms of both quality of output and the number of staff involved.

At the same time the objective is to maintain and enhance the quality of teaching and learning. The faculty enjoys a strong reputation as a provider of vocational education. An emphasis on student skills development and the involvement of employers in courses has long been a feature of many programmes. Such features of course design are now the focus of the wider debate in higher education, stimulated by the Enterprise in Higher Education programme and other initiatives.

In the past the recruitment practice, for staff, reflected the emphasis placed on industrial experience and business-related skills. Many staff, the author included, have not followed the more traditional academic route to becoming a lecturer, which normally includes an 'apprenticeship' in research. The increased emphasis on research therefore created a need for a staff development programme.

The approach to staff development, described here, was against this background of:

● an increased emphasis on research and publication;

● the different starting points of staff in terms of research expertise and level of interest;

● the need to balance research activity against the continuing objectives of delivering quality teaching to an increasing number of students;

● the recognition that including something in institutional/faculty/departmental objectives doesn't automatically make it happen!

Like most changes this one wasn't universally welcomed, or understood, and the degree of individual enthusiasm and support clearly varied.

STAFF DEVELOPMENT STRATEGY

Within the institution, responsibility for staff development is largely devolved to departments. Each has responsibility for the development of individuals and groups of staff, to meet its overall curriculum and research objectives. In the case of research-related staff development it was agreed that there should also be activities at faculty level in order to meet the high-priority objective of raising the research profile.

The task of coordinating the faculty initiatives was taken on by Ardha

Danieli, a senior research fellow, and myself. I had managed the Enterprise in Higher Education programme since 1988 so had experience of managing change in higher education and of organizing responsive staff development. Also, as a manager who career-changed to education, I was well aware of the different language and culture which seemed to surround research. Ardha, on the other hand, has a strong background in social science research, is well-versed in its ways, and has experience of teaching research methodology and supervision. We have found that this combination of different backgrounds and experience has been really helpful in planning this initiative. To some extent we represent the different traditions of academics in the faculty and our plans reflect these different perspectives.

This chapter focuses on initiatives at faculty level, since 1992. Staff from all departments have taken part. By working closely with departmental research coordinators we feel we have been able to make the most of the resources available and to keep duplication of effort to a minimum.

Broad aims

Our main aims regarding this initiative are summarized below:

● to stimulate debate across the faculty about research and the implications of raising the profile of research and publications;

● to dispel some 'myths' and 'mystique' which can be seen to surround research – especially for those with little or no previous experience. Here we were conscious of the fact that the language used by those familiar with research, funding councils, refereed journals, etc., was quite foreign to some staff;

● to involve staff in identifying their own development needs, in order to engage in research, at a number of levels. This was seen as a vital part of our approach. Our aim was to allow for a wide variety of different starting points;

● to encourage staff to 'share' skills and knowledge. Here the aim was to stimulate ongoing collaboration between groups of staff, across departmental boundaries, and to make the most of the many talents in research and other areas;

● to provide a supportive environment for staff new to research.

Methods adopted

To address the issues and objectives above we developed a number of related activities which are described briefly below:

- *Faculty seminars.* These sought to cover broad areas about research and to stimulate debate across the faculty. The topics included, 'What is research?', Research – how to get started', 'Writing for publication'. These proved to be popular, well-attended events which certainly got people talking and highlighted other areas of development need/ interest.

- *Research skills course.* This programme of eight three-hour sessions on research methodology and methods has also proved to be attractive to staff and clearly meets a very real need. In 1992/3 the course was run five times (eight staff per course). In 1993/4 three further courses were run.

- *Specific development activities to meet staff demands.* Discussions with staff following the seminars and the research skills courses highlighted specific areas of interest for further development. These included, 'writing research proposals', 'computer-based literature searches', 'using statistics' and 'using information technology'. We circulated a note to all staff asking them to highlight their own areas of interest. Over 60 staff indicated interest and a programme of suitable sessions was developed for 1993/4 and 1994/5.

- *Faculty doctoral programme.* Staff have been encouraged to register for MPhil or PhD higher degrees. This programme provides a one-year part-time methodology programme and peer support. This has provided staff with further training in social research methodology and also, through the increased number of higher degree students, helped to raise the profile of research.

- *Departmental research seminars.* Support has been given to extend the range of seminars and opening them up to all interested faculty staff. All departments now have an active programme of seminars. These provide a forum for staff, including those new to research and higher degree students, to present their work to peers for comment and criticism.

PROGRESS TO DATE – ISSUES FOR THE FUTURE

Over 120 staff have participated in one aspect of this initiative or another. Indeed some staff have taken part in all aspects. Demand is high for further developments. Despite many other pressures and priorities staff are finding the time to take part in these activities. To some extent this response reflects the high institutional priority given to research, which is reinforced through the individual review system. However, feedback so far suggests that the range of activities offered have helped to provide a high level of support, encouragement and relevant knowledge/skills for staff.

Clearly it is early days yet for this and other initiatives which seek to raise the level of research activity in the faculty. In the short term our aim is to meet the demand for development which we have helped to identify and stimulate. Each activity highlights further, often more specific, needs. To meet these we are drawing on expertise from across the faculty and beyond. In the longer term our aim is to continue to respond to staff needs as the level of research activity rises.

A number of lessons have been learnt so far which will influence our future plans and which may provide useful pointers for others engaged in or considering similar initiatives, these are highlighted below:

- Staff have *very* different starting points in terms of expertise, experience, enthusiasm, confidence, aims and expectations. Creating a climate which encourages questions at all levels is, we feel, vital if staff are to be encouraged to engage in research.

- In the short term raising the level of debate and stimulating demand for staff development has been relatively easy. In the longer term the growth in research activity clearly has wider implications including pressures on staff time and the need for a balance with other priorities.

- We need to consider how best to provide ongoing professional support for staff on individual and collaborative research projects in the future. Also we need to look more closely at the different roles which staff may fulfil on projects and associated skills development needs.

- Staff development is one important aspect of raising the research profile. The initiative described in this paper was part of an overall management strategy, and not dealt with in isolation. By operating at faculty level we have been able to work alongside other related developments, for example, an increase in internally-funded research projects and the appointment of ESRC teaching fellows. This type of coordination may not be easy where staff development is organized centrally in an institution.

Overall we feel that this staff development initiative has made a strong contribution towards raising the research profile of the faculty. Other changes in the broader picture in higher education will no doubt emerge. Each change will have implications for staff and for staff development and our experience here will inform our future staff development strategy.

Chapter 12

What Makes a Good Lecturer in Higher Education? Outcomes of a SCED/SEDA Small-Grant Project

Sally Brown, Dorothy Bell and Liz McDowell

INTRODUCTION

What makes a good lecturer? And for that matter, what makes a good staff developer? These were the key questions we set out to address in our SCED/SEDA small-grant funded research. We were awarded the grant to investigate lecturers' perceptions of effective teaching in higher education, using repertory grid techniques and to develop a toolkit to enable staff and educational developers to use repertory grid techniques in their development and training work.

The team consists of Liz McDowell, who has a background in evaluation and research, Sally Brown, who is an active workshop facilitator and writer on educational issues in higher education and Dorothy Bell, who has a background in psychology. We all work in the Educational Development Service of the University of Northumbria at Newcastle (UNN). We have also drawn on the expertise of Dr. Delia Wakelin, a lecturer in psychology at UNN who has advised on the statistical processing of the data we have obtained.

WHY REPERTORY GRIDS?

The repertory grid approach is based on Kelly's (1963) personal construct theory. It can be used both to elicit personal constructs and also to facilitate discussion and negotiation of shared constructs within a group. The potential use of the technique to enable individuals to refine and share their constructs is particularly valuable to staff and educational developers. Many development and training programmes aim to enable participants to make their personal concepts and perspectives on teaching more explicit, to become more aware of other views and to begin a process of developing and refining their own personal theories. For example, the SEDA Accreditation Scheme for teachers in HE places considerable emphasis on teachers being able to make explicit their values in relation to learning and teaching, scholarship, working with colleagues and professional development.

Despite their potential usefulness, repertory grids have been little used in higher education, the exception being the work of Zuber-Skerritt (1989, 1991) in Australia.

PILOT STUDY

As we wished to develop our methodology to make it appropriate for our own particular context, we decided to pilot it with ourselves and academic colleagues in the Educational Development Service, UNN. This gave us seven subjects and for this part of the work it seemed most appropriate to ask, 'What makes a good staff/educational developer?' rather than 'lecturer'.

Using the pilot study repertory grids (see Figure 12.1), we asked our colleagues to think about six staff developers (represented as elements on the grid), the first themselves, the second their ideal self as a staff developer, the third a good staff developer known to them, the fourth a poor staff developer known to them, the fifth another good staff developer and the last another poor one. Although we encouraged them to think of actual people and to write initials on the grid so they could always recall who they were thinking about, these identities were kept confidential to the subject. It is an important part of the repertory grid approach that the interviewee focuses on specific people (or events or objects). This is to discourage them from making very generalized statements and giving the answers they think would be most acceptable, and to encourage them to reveal the ways in which they really do distinguish between, in our case, effective and ineffective lecturers or staff developers. The distinction we are making here relates closely to the notions of 'espoused theory' and 'theory-in-use' proposed by Argyris and Schön, (1974).

Usually two of us did the interviews, with Dorothy keeping to fairly tightly scripted questions and Liz or Sally acting as note-taker. Typically, Dorothy would ask for each line on the grid: 'Looking at these three staff developers, indicated by the "0" in the column, how are two of them similar in terms of their effectiveness as staff developers, and how do they differ from the third?' She would encourage the subject to summarize the response in a few words and these would be recorded verbatim in the boxes for emergent constructs (the things two had in common) and

	Elements						
Emergent Constructs With their attributes as Lecturers in mind, what do the pair have in common?	Self as a Lecturer E1	The Lecturer I want to become E2	A good Lecturer E3	A not so good Lecturer E4	A good Lecturer E5	A not so good Lecturer E6	**Implicit Constructs** With their attributes as Lecturers in mind, what makes the other Lecturer different?
1	0	0	0				
2				0	0	0	
3	0		0		0		
4		0		0		0	
5			0	0		0	
6			0		0	0	
7		0	0	0			
8	0		0			0	

Figure 12.1 *Pilot study repertory grids*

implicit constructs (the things that make the third different). These were not always exact opposites, as our results show. The note-taker took longer notes so that we could check our accuracy later, but otherwise kept silent.

Having identified bi-polar constructs, these were then transferred to the rating scale grid (see Figure 12.2) and each person was asked to rate each element (staff developer) on a scale one to five, with one being greatest similarity to the construct and five being very similar to the opposite end of the construct. At this point we added an additional construct, 'effective-ineffective', and asked interviewees to rate each element on this construct too.

	Elements					
CONSTRUCTS 1 = very similar 5 = not similar at all	E1 Self as Lecturer	E2 The Lecturer I want to become	E3 A good Lecturer	E4 A not so good Lecturer	E5 A good Lecturer	E6 A not so good Lecturer
1 1 = 5 =						
2 1 = 5 =						
3 1 = 5 =						
4 1 = 5 =						
5 1 = 5 =						
6 1 = 5 =						
7 1 = 5 =						
8 1 = 5 =						
9 1 =Effective 5 = Ineffective						

This rating scale method is to express relationships between elements and constructs.

On a scale of 1 - 5 allocate to each element a number between 1 and 5

1 = element is very similar to construct   5 = very similar to the opposite end of the construct

Figure 12.2 *Rating scale*

Bi-polarity relies on constructs being defined by the ways in which both constructs and the people differ from each other. Our thinking on this has been informed by critical theorists like Derrida (1967), who suggests that meaning is itself constructed through the 'free play of the signifier', that is, the way in which signification becomes meaningful to us in the active differences we perceive between opposites. This is not always entirely helpful however, because in many cases it is not easy to juxtapose two opposites, as often a better way is to position concepts on a continuum rather than at opposite ends of an artificial scale.

In our research it was sometimes the case that our interviewees gave us constructs that were diametrically opposed. For example, one construct, 'reliability', had the obvious opposite, 'unreliability'. However, the construct, 'warm, caring about people' has as its opposed construct, 'self-interest'. Here we can perceive the flavour of the thinking, but these constructs are not always just simple opposites of each other.

The set of constructs we obtained were very varied in terms of the way that they were expressed, revealing individual nuances in the way that effectiveness was construed, but also revealing clear themes or areas of effectiveness, which were considered to be significant by all of our interviewees.

Communication skills, organizational skills and interpersonal skills were considered to be relevant to the effectiveness of staff developers. Since these generic skills appear in lists of qualities required in many professional contexts this is perhaps unsurprising. Personal qualities such as self-esteem, confidence and a sense of personal security were also mentioned and might be considered part of these generic requirements. However, they may be particularly important for the staff developer who is a change agent, as was revealed by a number of constructs concerning reactivity/proactivity, strategic behaviour and vision.

In addition to being a professional, the educational or staff developer in higher education is also an academic and there were constructs which revealed this, mentioning the use of theory, ability to research and ability to publish. However, quite what the academic base of the work was did not emerge, except for a few constructs which mentioned being aware of the latest developments in HE and being knowledgeable about educational technology.

The remaining small cluster of constructs were about the values and beliefs of staff developers. For example, for some interviewees effectiveness as a staff developer was linked to a commitment to working at the grassroots, or to a focus on the improvement of student learning as a fundamental principle. A number of interviewees indicated that a commitment to being a staff developer and a clear philosophy of practice were related to effectiveness.

The statistical analysis of the data revealed how each individual's constructs clustered together, but we were most concerned to share constructs, and perhaps develop a consensus about the qualities related to effectiveness as a staff developer. To help us to share ideas and develop a model of effectiveness we decided to use hexagonal thinking. The *Thinking with Hexagons User Manual*, (IDON, 1992), describes how this creative problem-solving device can be used to help cluster similar ideas. We printed up all the constructs, attached them to hexagons with the intention of grouping them in ways that seemed to make sense of similar kinds of constructs, then labelled the groups with appropriate umbrella headings. At a meeting of all seven staff developers involved in the study we were able to use the hexagons in this way. A colleague, interested by the methodology, subsequently used the hexagons to develop an individual model.

When the constructs were clustered, similar groupings to those indicated above emerged. There was a general consensus that a range of interpersonal and personal skills were needed to be an effective staff developer, and other areas such as the ability to promote change and the need to function as an academic were also indicated. Two groupings of constructs not proposed above, also emerged. One grouping contained constructs to do with creativity, liveliness, enthusiasm and quick thinking. These were considered to be related to effectiveness for staff developers. The second grouping was related to the staff developer's role as a change agent within an organization and it was to do with knowledge of the specific organization in which the staff developer worked and their abilities to exert influence within the organization.

In more general terms, the consideration and grouping of constructs led to some interesting discussions. It appeared that an effective staff developer needed a very wide range of skills, knowledge and abilities and we discussed to what extent each individual staff developer needs all of these or whether different members of a team can contribute in particular areas. We realized that at UNN we are fortunate to work within a team, whereas many staff developers work alone. It was a matter of concern to some members of the group that many of the skills and attributes being discussed were very general and could be considered to be appropriate to many professionals or managers. There is an emphasis on generic skills in current thinking about education and training, and perhaps we are tending to overemphasize these at the expense of the specific skills and knowledge needed for particular specialisms.

We had difficulties in relating some of our constructs to the general notion of effectiveness as a staff developer. We felt that some skills and attributes might be needed for effectiveness in some contexts but not in others. Staff and educational developers work with individuals and with groups, in informal situations and in contexts such as training sessions and formal meetings. One conclusion might be that there was a construct missing from our extensive list which was to do with abilities to adapt to different contexts and behave appropriately.

THE MAIN STUDY

Concurrently with the pilot study, as we developed each stage of the process, we then applied it to our sample group of 16 lecturers. We selected eight from each of two disciplines, Built Environment and

Business Studies. We chose these disciplines because these are not extensively covered by other research on lecturers' concepts and theories of teaching. In each case, four of these were relatively new lecturers on our Postgraduate Certificate in Educational Development course and four were more experienced lecturers.

Our methodology was identical to that which we used with staff developers except that, in this case, Dorothy undertook all the interviews on her own. We used repertory grids identical to those used in the pilot, but with 'lecturer' replacing 'staff developer'. We did make a small amendment to the grid, replacing the word 'poor' with the words 'not so good'. Interviewees seemed unhappy about designating someone they knew as a poor lecturer or staff developer but the words 'not so good' seemed to be more acceptable to them. At the time of writing, we have completed all the interviews, analysed the data and are currently organising the discipline specific discussions using hexagons. The findings from the main study will form part of a later publication.

One thing that was noticeable was that people from the two different disciplines approached this in very different ways. The lecturers in the Built Environment took longer over the task and they had little familiarity with the processes we were using. The Business School participants had an acquaintance with general applications of this kind of research. Both groups generally commented that they found it difficult to decide whether their colleagues were good or bad, other than by hearsay, because they tend not to sit in on each other's teaching. Some mentioned that they made judgements based on what they heard from students in off-the-cuff remarks. Our participants often have quite ambivalent and conflicting views about what makes a good lecturer, not having clear and explicit criteria on which to base judgements.

A preliminary content analysis of the constructs obtained, without at this stage trying to distinguish between disciplines and between new and experienced lecturers, has been carried out. The largest number of constructs were concerned with presentation and communication skills. However almost as many constructs about the lecturer's relationship with students emerged. Effective lecturers were considered to be approachable, concerned about students and willing to spend time with them.

Most participants gave one or two constructs relating to organizational skills such as time management, good preparation and contribution to departmental tasks. The need to have relevant and up-to-date knowledge and expertise, sometimes including good professional contacts, was similarly mentioned by most participants. The grouping of constructs relating to commitment to teaching was almost as large but derived from a smaller number of participants. While some did not raise this issue, others did have the view that effective lecturers were interested and committed to teaching whereas ineffective ones were uninterested, unenthusiastic and perhaps more interested in research.

The remaining groupings of constructs were derived from a minority of participants. Some mentioned the need for lecturers to have a variety of techniques and approaches at their disposal and to be willing to try out new things and be innovative in their teaching. Assessment of students was mentioned, particularly the prompt return to students of assessed work. There were a small number of constructs which related to the type of teaching and learning which an effective lecturer would engage in. Opinions varied here. For example, for one participant, an effective lecturer would promote student-centred learning and avoid feeding students with information, whereas for another an effective lecturer would make sure that students went away with a good set of notes.

OUTCOMES

As well as gaining some interesting insights into what people think makes good staff developers and lecturers, we anticipate that our research will enable us to produce a tool kit for use with our own new lecturers and for external dissemination to help colleagues examine, particularly with new staff, some of the underlying assumptions that people hold about lecturing (the outcomes of the pilot work on staff/educational development will form the basis of different articles and activities). At a workshop at Preston in September 1993, we described our preliminary work and the participants there encouraged us to believe that the methodology will have an extremely wide range of uses, wider indeed than we had originally envisaged. They suggested using the approach with new staff, academic or administrative, with heads of department or senior managers, with students, especially adult learners, or other clients. It was suggested that it might help people to think about questions such as, 'What is a manager?' and might help with team-building or inducting a new team member.

THE SEDA CONFERENCE WORKSHOP, NOVEMBER 1993

This workshop provided us with the opportunity to share with a wider audience our methodology and our preliminary findings. Modelling the processes in extremely truncated forms, we were able to give a flavour of the techniques and to elicit further comments and reactions. These will be helpful to us in the ultimate production of the tool kit for subsequent use.

This chapter describes work in progress; we anticipate finishing the research early in 1994. We are very grateful to SCED/SEDA for providing us with the impetus to start this work, which we have found enjoyable and most informative. As we are still at a stage of work in progress, we would welcome comments, advice and reactions from colleagues outside UNN to help us further refine and develop our work.

REFERENCES

Argyris, C and Schön, D A (1974) *Theory in Practice*, San Francisco, CA: Jossey-Bass.

Derrida, J (1967) *'L'Ecriture et la difference'*, Paris Seuil, trans Alan Bass, *Writing and Difference*, University of Chicago Press.

IDON (1992) *Thinking with Hexagons User Manual*, Pitlochry, IDON Magnetics Ltd.

Kelly, G A (1963) *A Theory of Personality*, New York: Norton.

Zuber-Skerrit, O (1989) 'Case study: personal constructs of second language teaching', *Educational and Training Technology International*, 26, 1, 60–67.

Zuber-Skerritt, O (1991) 'Eliciting personal constructs of research, teaching and/or professional development', *International Journal of Qualitative Studies in Education*, 4, 4, 333–40.

Chapter 13

Towards a Model of the Learner in Higher Education: Some Implications for Teachers

Mike O'Neil

INTRODUCTION: 'DEEP' AND 'SURFACE' LEARNING

The model of the learner that I believe higher education should aspire to in fostering high quality learning is essentially one embracing the principles of adult learning (eg, Knowles, 1978; Rogers, 1983) and heeding the findings of recent research into student learning as well as the wisdom arising from the practice of teaching (eg, Entwistle, 1992; Gibbs, 1992; Ramsden, 1992).

Research over the past ten or so years has revealed a distinction between 'deep' and 'surface' approaches to learning on the part of students in post-16 education. This distinction is essentially one between meaningful ('deep') learning and rote ('surface') learning. A 'surface' approach is characterized as an attempt to complete in a minimal way the task requirements so as to maximize the rewards of learning; that is, the grades or marks given by teachers. In this form of learning, tasks are viewed as an external imposition and students are generally unreflective about purposes and/or strategies. Memorizing information, in order to satisfy assessment criteria narrowly focusing on reproduction, is the dominant mode of learning.

A 'deep' approach, adopted by students who seek to make sense of subject content through a vigorous interaction with it, captures the essence of academic life as I understand it. Here the intention is to relate new ideas to old and to everyday experience as much as to relate evidence to conclusions. Meaning is sought during every academic encounter by examining, amongst other things, the logic of arguments, the plausibility of evidence, and the conceptual and methodological framework of the discipline studied. In other words, the majority of learning resulting from a *higher* education should be 'deep' by definition.

The principles which follow might be used as a menu by individual lecturers (for informing and developing their approach to teaching) or by course teams (in developing a teaching-learning strategy for a new course). In both instances, there would be a long-term commitment to setting up a learning-teaching environment that fosters a 'deep' approach to study.

EIGHT PRINCIPLES FOR ENHANCING HIGH QUALITY LEARNING IN UNIVERSITIES AND COLLEGES

1. Enhancing student capabilities and work-related skills

Enhancing student qualities such as self-reliance, intellectual capabilities and intrinsic interest in learning are important aims of higher education. Among the most significant facets of this principle are:

- encouraging learners to be self-reliant and to develop independent modes of learning, eg:
  - group work and projects which stress learning contracts
  - projects and enquiries requiring skills of independent study and autonomy of action
  - setting up learning tasks placing a demand on teachers to 'let go' of their control over what is taught and how it is taught
  - identifying the specific skills needed in work placement
  - planning and implementing tasks/projects within a work-related context
  - setting up learning tasks/projects which enable students to plan and manage time effectively
  - providing opportunities for considered reflection on work experience and the communication of that in clear analytical language;

- developing students' personal qualities, eg
  - self-esteem (helping students to develop a positive self-image and building up students' confidence)
  - intellectual capabilities (abilities to analyse and evaluate issues and problems)
  - specialist knowledge as well as personal transferable skills;

- enabling the most socially useful type of learning to occur; that is, learning how to learn, where lifelong learning is the primary goal, eg:
  - attempting to cultivate intrinsic interest in learning for its own sake
  - being committed to research, scholarship and critical enquiry
  - developing study and information-processing skills

- being willing to experiment with new ideas and practices
- raising awareness of techniques for the effective management of tasks, time and people
- enabling students to recognize their personal strengths and weaknesses, interests and needs and how to capitalize on these
- simulating work and other social situations in which students can practise developing strategies for solving problems without undue fear of failure.

2. Using student experience as a learning resource

Students have valuable experience and knowledge which needs to be built upon by universities. The most significant features of this principle in my view are as follows:

- acknowledging and using students' experiences as a valuable learning resource, eg:
    - encouraging opportunities for experiential learning
    - fostering syndicate group work and the sharing of ideas and experiences through critical friends' groups
    - accepting students' present level of knowledge and experience as a starting point for development
    - using current strengths and interests of group members to enhance the learning process
    - using student perceptions as a means of listing research concepts and methodologies;
- establishing learning contexts where learners feel that full recognition is given to setting objectives that match their own purposes, needs and level of prior achievements and accomplishments, eg:
    - negotiating learning to meet individual needs and interests (an 'open' curriculum)
    - sequentially developing learning activities based on the learner's previous learning (a 'spiral' curriculum)
    - providing academic and personal tutoring as an integral part of courses, and more explicit educational guidance for informed choice in, say, a modular system;
- ensuring that learning tasks and activities are relevant to learners' personal and professional development, eg:
    - determining learner's aspirations and ambitions and building learning tasks around this agenda
    - signalling that not all learning material will be perceived as

immediately relevant to the learner but demonstrating its connection in some way or another with the world of work
- embedding personal and work-related skills in courses, for example group work, IT skills, presentation skills, foreign languages, etc.
- providing careers education as a standard component for all students
- ensuring a continuing contact with employers to make sure that the course remains relevant to their needs.

3. Encouraging active and cooperative learning

Another feature of my outlook is the value of sharing and mutual support: exchanging views but also working cooperatively and caringly. In other words, I attach major importance to the social and emotional climate in which I work and in which I expect my students to work. I see myself in partnership with students. I also know that learning is most influential if it is done actively rather than passively. I believe these qualities will be promoted by:

- providing a supportive and cooperative learning environment, eg:
  - establishing 'active' approaches to learning in seminars and workshops, for example pyramid group discussion and syndicate groups
  - setting up self-help groups and tutorless groups
  - encouraging assessment of group work as well as of individual projects
  - setting up cooperative learning contexts among staff and students, for example production of a portfolio
  - establishing systems for more extensive and formal support for the acquisition of effective study skills
  - providing for the greater use of, say, student-managed workbooks to support key lectures;
- making sure that learners are active during learning sessions, where learners reflect upon their experience and relate this experience to theoretical models and explanations, eg:
  - ensuring that learners are aware of the logic of 'active' learning by exercises calculated to show the power of 'deep' compared with 'surface' learning
  - encouraging students regularly to record their course experience and developing thinking in a portfolio and periodically to hold review meetings where the exchange of ideas and experiences arising from the portfolio occurs

- varying the mode of teaching and learning activities to avoid boredom on the part of students (and staff?).

4. Promoting responsibility in learning

It is important that students come to accept responsibility for their actions. To do so represents a recognition that we live in a social world and that our actions have consequences for other people. It is also vital that students come to feel in control of their learning and their development and, to this end, students should be given opportunities for self-managed projects and for self-constructed modules. So, I believe that teachers should:

- create a teaching-learning climate that enables individuals to participate responsibly in the learning process, eg:
  - allowing learners to take responsibility for determining what, when and how they learn in formal as well as informal settings
  - fostering opportunities for students to be sensitive to their responsibilities and duties, to recognize the needs of others and to listen to others
  - encouraging students to exchange ideas with peers and tutors
  - encouraging students to make effective use of human/material resources;
- provide curricula that are flexible and enable learners to make meaningful choices in terms of subject content, programme routes, approaches to assessment, and modes and duration of study, eg:
  - providing more open and resource-based learning, including text-based work books
  - enabling students to access modular course menus *and* the financial/administrative procedures which accommodate discontinuity of study
  - allowing students greater use of 'elective' modules from a cross-institutional menu
  - allowing students to determine the appropriate assessment for a module/topic area.

5. Engaging with feelings, values and motives as well as with intellectual development

This has a particular connection with the value which I place on students as people. This principle has a number of implications:

- providing learning opportunities and encounters which involve the whole person: feelings, values and motives as well as intellect, eg:
  - attempting to convey enthusiasm for the area of activity
  - conveying a sense of a joint endeavour in the pursuit of understanding
  - encouraging risk-taking and minimizing anxiety about errors (learning from mistakes)
  - compiling a portfolio in which progress in learning is documented /reflected upon /acted upon
  - providing experiences which show that learning in this subject is (can be) fun
  - encouraging students to self-evaluate through making judgements about quality of work and highlighting moments of achievement
  - enabling students to articulate and debate their own value systems.

6. Fostering open, flexible and outcomes-based assessment

Assessment on courses should be conducted within a framework where open, reflexive and outcomes-based processes are evident:

- assessing learning through self-, peer- and teacher-assessment processes, where the criteria are made explicit following negotiation with students, eg:
  - encouraging syndicate group members to provide formal and informal feedback to each other (inter- and intra-group)
  - establishing a framework for critique of an assignment or project report through group-based discussion
  - using a set of indicative assessment criteria as a framework for negotiation with students;
- assessment strategies should be congruent with clearly defined learning outcomes which recognize and credit student achievement, eg:
  - adopting a wider range of approaches to assessment than is currently the case, including Records of Achievement which contain transcripts and materials from portfolios
  - re-presenting course documentation to emphasize what students will know, understand and be able to do at the end of a sequence of teaching. Teaching methods would be directed towards securing these learning outcomes (cf. Entwistle, 1992; Otter, 1992);
- assessment strategies should be cost-effective in terms of large group sizes and should complement the development of autonomy in learning, eg:

- much wider use of 'cost-effective' modes of assessment, for example multiple-choice formats capable of being read by an optical scanner, and systems for the self-assessment of student projects.

7. Evaluating teaching and learning

A prime condition for effective learning is a commitment on the part of university teachers to reflect on their own practice with a view to improving it so as to enhance the quality of the student learning experience. This I take minimally to include collecting evidence from the key participants (self, colleagues, students) by using a variety of evaluation instruments and processes on a number of occasions as a course develops. The ethos is very much that of a 'reflective practitioner' (Schön, 1983) using tools of evaluation data collection associated with triangulation (O'Neil and Pennington, 1992).

Furthermore, it is self-evident that institutions need to establish an institutional climate which values student involvement in the evaluation of teaching and the assessment of learning (see NUS, 1992, and Partington *et al.*, 1993). Such an involvement would mean, amongst other things, that institutions would need to:

- develop student skills in giving feedback
- set up more standard and systematic approaches to module and programme evaluation (some supported by IT)
- encourage and cajole staff to create a 'customer satisfaction' culture and to develop the notion of service standards (possibly through a mutually agreed two-way contract with students).

8. Establishing congruence between learning and teaching activities and the milieu in which they occur

Provision of a physical and material environment is supportive of learning and is appropriate for the activities involved, eg:

- adequate library and computing resources
- speedy access to word-processing and photocopying resources
- better equipped teaching spaces and mass lecture rooms with a wider range of more sophisticated presentational equipment
- appropriate 'open' learning support and spaces.

Author's note: This chapter develops some ideas first described in Nightingale and O'Neil (1994).

Acknowledgement: My thanks to the participants in my workshop at the SEDA Conference, Cardiff, November 1993 who suggested additional ideas for some of the principles listed in this chapter.

REFERENCES

Entwistle, N (1992) *The Impact of Teaching on Learning Outcomes in Higher Education*, Sheffield: CVCP/Universities' Staff Development Unit.

Gibbs, G (1992) *Improving the Quality of Student Learning*, Bristol: Technical and Educational Services.

Knowles, M (1978) *The Adult Learner: A neglected species*, Houston, Tx: Gulf Publishing.

Nightingale, P and O'Neil, M (1994) *Achieving Quality Learning in Higher Education*, London: Kogan Page.

NUS (1992) *NUS Student Charter*, London: National Union of Students.

O'Neil, M J and Pennington, R C (1992) *Evaluating Teaching and Courses from an Active Learning Perspective*, Sheffield: CVCP/ USDU.

Otter, S (1992) *Learning Outcomes in Higher Education*, London: HMSO.

Partington, P *et al.* (1993) *Student Feedback: Context, issues and practice*, Sheffield: CVCP/ Universities' Staff Development Unit.

Ramsden, P (1992) *Learning to Teach in Higher Education*, London: Routledge.

Rogers, C (1983) *Freedom to Learn for the 80s*, London: Merrill.

Schön, D A (1983) *The Reflective Practitioner: How professionals think in action*, London: Temple Smith.

Chapter 14

The Accreditation of Work-based Research: An Action Research/ Action Learning Model

Michael Gregory

INTRODUCTION

'Action research' and 'action learning' each has a literature promoting itself as both a methodology for the professional practitioner to improve practice and as a technique that may be used to educate. Although having a common thread, the research on each tends generally to be exclusive to itself, and an examination of the literature reveals that there are essential distinctions, as well as a confluence in the processes involved. This must be borne in mind in using action research and action learning in post-graduate curriculum design. Despite action research being most commonly associated with the development of teachers, and action learning with management development, there is no reason why the approaches cannot be employed generically with other groups of professionals. In fact, action research and action learning may be extremely relevant ways in which to build upon both postgraduate and post-experiential qualifications, particularly in a mass higher education market which is organizing into flexible and portable credit accumulation and transfer and where consumers are looking for educational opportunities offering not only academic challenge but enquiry directly related to the world of work.

THE REFLECTIVE PROFESSIONAL

Elliott (1991) has recently outlined what he terms the 'reflective practitioner model of professionalism', and calls for professional education to be essentially experiential, involving the study of real practical situations, with a pedagogy underpinning the capacity for competent reflective practice and where knowledge acquisition provides a framework of understanding around which reflection can build on workplace reality (p.314). It was this vision which influenced the design of the new Master of Arts degree in Human Resource Strategy (HRS) developed jointly by Suffolk College of Higher Education – an Associate College of the University of East Anglia (UEA) – and UEA itself.

This collaboration, the key aim of which was to offer an accreditation opportunity for human resource practitioners or for line managers with significant human resource management responsibilities, involved academics from the university's Centre for Applied Research in Education (CARE) and teaching staff from the Institute of Personnel Management (IPM) Centre of Excellence based in the college's School of Educational and Administrative Studies. The design team itself was carefully matched to bring together higher education teachers and researchers who had been involved in delivering both a traditional professional curriculum and who also had experience of action research and action learning approaches and who themselves were enthusiastic about the use of collaborative action research in developing both curriculum and themselves as professionals.

The notion of bringing these people and methodologies together to deliver a work-based learning approach for an MA in Human Resource Strategy seeking to 'provide human resource professionals with the capability and confidence to influence strategic decision-making' (validation document, p.1) was an exciting challenge, particularly in attempting to reconcile the tensions that have existed between proponents of action learning and action researchers. Reg Revans, who 'invented' action learning, is actually quite impatient of some features of action research such as the emphasis on the collection of data, analysis of data and writing/publication of case studies. Those who work in an action research paradigm are equally suspicious of action learning, particularly the degree of subscription often held by action learning proponents of theory. Some, as in the MA team, are attracted to the action group learning idea and the notion of teacher as facilitator, but think that the approach to problem solving is much too elementary, relying too heavily on a simple notion of cause and effect. The key aim of the research in constructing the programme methodology was therefore to synthesize the two approaches into a distinctive curriculum which centred on developing the reflective and action-oriented human resource practitioner working or aspiring to work in a strategic role, and whilst there is an implicit challenge in the pedagogy of the MA programme to a traditionally concerted management development programme, we have included provision for 'critical input' at key points.

A primary reason for developing an 'action' approach to curriculum delivery was the very nature of action research and action learning itself. The essential requirement was to tailor an advanced developmental programme for professionals who could bring their own expertise and who, by researching their own practice, would be able to improve performance at work and make what Halsey (1972) has described as 'intervention in the functioning of the real world', particularly in the organizations that employ them. This fundamental aim was incorporated in the course philosophy: '...the course will be ... a research degree incorporating a substantial element, with an emphasis on practical relevance to the workforce' (validation document, p.l).

DEFINING ACTION RESEARCH AND ACTION LEARNING

An immediate issue for the design team was to actually decide on what it meant by the two terms of 'action research' and 'action learning'. Zuber-Skerritt (1992) points out that action research is based on the 'fundamental concepts of action learning, adult learning and holistic dialectical thinking ... and on the principles of experiential learning and critical thinking' (p.88) and that action learning is 'a basic concept of action research' (p.214).

Action learning theory propounds that professionals will learn in the most effective way by focusing on actual organizational settings, within a supporting and challenging framework of enquiry by peer group interaction (Boisot and Fiol, 1987; Harries, 1991) and where personal empowerment can be encouraged through learner interdependency. It is about individuals learning from experience through reflection and action (McGill and Beaty, 1992), usually to solve problems at work. This process, which is individually focused, uses a learning group, known as a 'set', which provides a forum wherein the set members' ideas can be challenged within a supportive environment (see Figure 14.1).

Action learning emphasizes self-development and doing (MacNamara and Weekes, 1982) but this simplistic statement opens up an epistemology which is complex and sophisticated. The model put forward by its original guru, Reg Revans, was founded on assumptions similar to the four-stage experiential learning model (see Figure 14.2) developed by Lewin (1952) and Kolb (1984).

Revans' (1971) proposition of the learning process was set in the notion of scientific inquiry, and seemed to best fit the type of professional who was to be encouraged onto the MA degree: one who would want to learn by bearing responsibility for action. The concept involved in action learning was spelled out by Revans (1976, p.40) as:

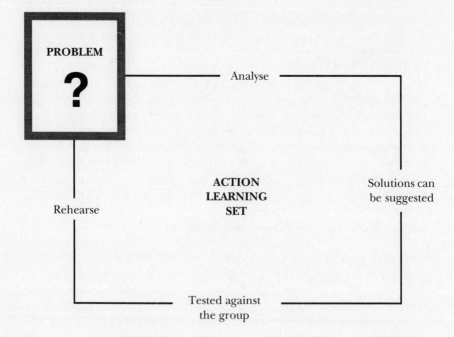

Figure 14.1   *The action learning group process*

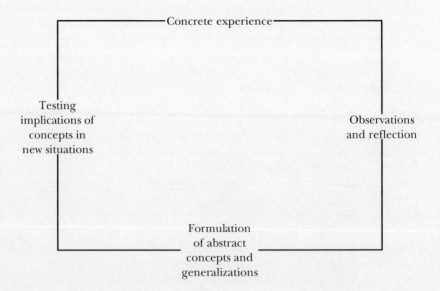

Figure 14.2   *Experiential learning model developed by Lewin*

- Men or women learn only when they want to learn

- One important reason for wanting to learn is an awareness of one's incapacity adequately to do one's job

- Learning is a social process, since involving each other in some problems of common interest, the learners help each other.

It involves a process which Boddy (1984) describes as an unending cycle of action, reflection and understanding, and the view subscribed to by the design team was that a learner at any level,

> can acquire knowledge through following a similar process of active search and research which specialist researchers undergo, rather than being taught and passively absorbing the results of their research (Zuber-Skerritt, 1992).

The aim was to avoid a 'course' which simply passed on knowledge and instead to create a learning process grounded in naturalistic research and which had a convexity towards what Revans (1983) called 'Q' – the acquisition of ability to ask fresh questions, to cope with new problems and deal with changing situations. (See Figure 14.3).

MATCHING ACTION AND RESEARCH

The intention was to turn the course participant into an agent for change in the organization which was to be researched, and this requires a research approach which is not only oriented towards action, but one which is deliberate, rigorous and public. Action research, as a form of applied social research which could draw together theory and action, matched intentions in that it can facilitate both advances in theory and effect social change through a process outlined by Kemmis (1988) as a

Figure 14.3   *The 'learning' in action learning (Revans, 1983, p.11)*

spiral of continuous analysis, fact-finding, conceptualization, planning, execution, more fact-finding and evaluation.

ACCREDITATION ISSUES

The MA in Human Resource Strategy is designed to be a one-year programme and is structured to build upon the knowledge gained at Diploma level in either Personnel Management (DPM) or Management Studies (DMS). Giving an accreditation value of 70 'M' (Masters) level points to the DPM and DMS, the MA essentially provides an opportunity somewhere between a taught and a research degree (worth a further 50 CAT points) for experienced professionals to continue their own personal development. At least four years of experience is necessary to enter the programme, and because the learning is post-experiential, newly qualified graduates are channelled into the pre-entry Diploma level which is more traditionally structured. The approach represents a view that action learning is a methodology that can work with diversity, a point made by McGill and Beaty (1992), who indicate that the approach is highly appropriate for part-time study which is work-related and which can respond to the needs and changes in circumstance of the participants (p.199).

The method adopted also reflected a caution about the delivery of what has sometimes been seen as a 'quick fix' approach of competence-based education and training in management and professional development (Woodcock, 1991). While what was offered as an academic programme was by no means unique (McGill and Beaty, 1992; Thorpe, 1988; Thorpe and Taylor, 1991), the desire was to open up the programme and make it attractive to those practitioners who aspire to work in a model of professional practice similar to what Schön (1983) has characterized as the 'reflective practitioner', and what Elliott (1991) has recently outlined as possessing features including:

- collaboration with clients (individuals, groups, communities) in identifying, clarifying and resolving their problems;

- the importance of communication and empathy with clients as a means of understanding situations from their point of view;

- a new emphasis on the holistic understanding of situations as the basis for professional practice, rather than on understanding them exclusively in terms of a particular set of specialist categories;

- self-reflection as a means of overcoming stereotypical judgements and responses. (p.311).

This was addressed by the course design team through the crucial process of group learning which provides a powerful armoury for development:

> During the blocks of teaching, time will be allocated to discuss issues, share experience and facilitate each other's learning. This will provide an opportunity to challenge assumptions, question practice and develop further professional techniques. This shared learning activity will enable participants to gain a wider perspective of their specialism as well as developing their ability to work collaboratively and facilitate the work of peers. (Validation document, p.5)

DEVELOPING THE CHANGE AGENT

In effect, the conduct of the action research will be a vehicle for learning in order to act differently to some degree and the ensuing process of change will entail action and reflection within the cyclical framework (Wallace, 1987). The construct was to facilitate the MA participants to make inquiry leading to understanding; and to use that understanding as the basis for improvement. Action research matched this intention in that it aims to contribute both to the practical concerns of people in an immediate problematic situation and to the goals of social science by joint collaboration within a mutually acceptable ethical framework of research. Lewin's evaluation of action research as a form of social action leading to improvement suggested that this model of curriculum implementation has great value not only for student learning, but also for academics' own teaching and professional development as higher education teachers, and the ongoing process of course review and evaluation has taken an action-oriented form of research, with immediate value as a form of INSET as colleagues share experiences and challenge perceptions.

It was the aim therefore to create a programme where the manager-researcher was helped in his/her investigation by a supporting and facilitating framework of academic support, in effect synthesizing academic research and practitioner experience along a continuum from which the course participants could learn and develop by undertaking a substantive internal consultancy. The idea of action research also underpins the professionality of the practitioner and leads to empowerment. This is effected by being able to employ methods and procedures based on theoretical research and knowledge, particularly for testing and improving practice, and for establishing a sound rationale for what they are doing, and for building up confidence and resolution in changing things which may be causing dissatisfaction. By adopting a thinking, critical attitude towards his/her own practice, and testing research findings against others, the professional becomes not only a catalyst for change, but also autonomous and able to make independent judgements within his/her professional sphere (McNiff, 1988).

DELIVERY OF AN ACTION BASED DEGREE

The degree, which is assessed against a dissertation (of 15,000 words) based on the work-related investigation, operates in a traditional action learning mode. The duration of learning sets is over 12 months. Set sizes are a maximum of seven participants, and are facilitated by an experienced set adviser. Participants meet formally during workshops lasting for three days and these workshops meet residentially at regular intervals, six times during the 12-month period. The set members are encouraged to develop their network beyond formal meeting times, and can arrange to have non-facilitated set meetings between those sessions which have been programmed into the workshops. While all of the participants will have access to a specialist supervisor for their dissertation work, and each of the workshops has a themed focus related to a strategic issue in managing human resources, it was felt that input of a specialized nature should arise as identified by the students' own needs and requirements. Provision was made therefore for 'experts' whom the team preferred to define as critical thinkers (see Willmott, 1994, p.127) to be available to give lectures in specialized areas on topical issues; for panels of 'leading edge' practitioners and academics who can be 'interrogated' by students; seminars which may be either student- or expert-led; and 'think-tank' sessions which have senior practitioners as well as academics and students as members.

LEARNING PROCESSES

This structure reflects the concern that within an action research approach the learning process is itself different and engages the learner in a different level of experience – one that is emancipatory and critically reflective and which is transformative by helping the adult learners taking part to 'construe (their) experience in a way in which they can more clearly understand the reasons for their problems and understand the options open to them so that they may assume responsibility for decision-making' (Mezirow, 1981). It also recognizes the synergy created between theory and practice, what – in the educational context – Whitehead (1989) has termed a 'living form', rather than theory-led practice as advocated by Lewin or by theory generated from practice as propounded by Elliott (1991).

A fundamental issue was to establish that a one-year action research programme has quality in terms of being a respectable form of inquiry and that this is ensured by both academic rigour and real relevance in the workplace. The people recruited onto the programme have to be capable of constructing a project at a senior or strategic level, and possess or develop the influencing skills necessary to carry out the changes they propose; to ensure this, candidates were carefully evaluated using group and individual interviews and participative activities. This philosophy had fundamental implications for the team's approach to the learning process, and the programme is therefore structured around an 'active' rather than a passive approach. The learning sets themselves will provide a firm construct upon which the link between ideas and action can be engineered. As McGill and Beaty (1992) indicate, 'the function of the set is to enable set members to learn from the link between ideas and experience to generalise from the past and plan for the future' (p.205).

Candidates on the programme will hold a degree-level qualification and will demonstrate an ability to build on this by actually carrying out a strategic level project in their employing organization. Unwaged students will be helped to negotiate with local voluntary sector employers a practice setting where an investigation could be undertaken. What is intended is that the participants, through using theory to illuminate or describe the actions they have taken, will be equipped with the power to reflect and experiment on the outcomes of the project. It is an essential requirement that the student is able to implement the action that they are proposing, and this will require the development of their skills in working with other people in order to have an effect.

The approach taken embodies the view that professional development should be more overtly process-oriented rather than content-driven, and responds to Leavitt's (1972) call for such development programmes to be set in a multidimensional, unprogrammed problem-solving paradigm. The professional in contemporary and future organizations is working in a technically sophisticated environment, and knowledge of specialized areas and disciplines is both increasingly expansive and rapidly becomes redundant with new technology. The MA therefore mirrors what Zuber-Skerritt (1992) has heralded as a development process encompassing action research, action learning and process management which can provide a toolkit for the development of managers' and professionals' ability to utilize more general competences and methods in solving completely new problems and in fostering vision, entrepreneurial attitude and skills in collaborative working to compete within an increasingly global context (p.219–20).

ASSESSING ACTION RESEARCH AND ACTION LEARNING

A major issue was to rationalize exactly what it is that is being assessed within an accredited programme of action research. Certainly, the processes of action learning raise a challenge to an assessment system which in a university context is often 'controlled, implemented and validated separately from the learner' (McGill and Beaty, 1992); the important issue here is that the learning process itself is paramount: the conferment of a degree is simply an accreditation of outcomes which have been 'contracted' between the learner and the course team on entry. Students working towards the MA complete two short pieces of work, basically research preparation, and are summatively assessed on the quality of the final dissertation. They will also be encouraged to keep a journal which can be used to measure progress against original objectives. Review and evaluation of the programme will also be an important mechanism, not only for improving quality on the programme but as a means whereby students, through maintaining a record of their course experiences, can reflect on their own personal responsibility for action within a learning experience where the student is empowered and has a distinctive role alongside academics in curriculum implementation. The use of action research as a fundamental approach in curriculum delivery therefore had even greater significance in that it was also to be used as a means of developing and managing the course in a collaborative, action-oriented fashion.

MacNamara *et al.* (1990) point out that action-based Master's degrees do need to 'translate the often untidy and random learning experiences gained from the action learning phase into acceptable academic dissertations to meet the tidy and disciplined requirements of a Master's degree' (p.429) and there is a thorough initial induction process (which follows recruitment through an assessment centre approach). The course structure has a detailed pattern of set meetings, and there is a clear emphasis not only on the development of set working, but also on formal sessions to improve the research skills of participants, and to consider the ethical issues in research design.

Employers will be involved in the programme, and students will be expected to gain their organization's commitment to the project; there is an expectation that follow-up activities will take place with the 'client' organization to investigate the effects of the student's work in order to verify what the student has learned from the action research. As McGill and Beaty (1992) point out, assessment of action learning is integrated into a continual, process-oriented perspective, rather than a purely 'summative "snapshot" of attainment' (p.210).

IS ACTION LEARNING AND ACTION RESEARCH RESPECTABLE?

Because the course is based on the fundamental principle of action research and is centred on the individual's own systematic and evaluative inquiry into what is a unique circumstance, it does face the challenge of validity; a common view of action research is that this quality is lacking due to its inherent subjectivity, lack of universality and consequent unreliability.

Because the course methodology is geared to a qualitative perspective, and within that to an action research/action learning paradigm, there may be an inherent criticism that only a narrow and limited range of research skills are being acquired by the candidates, and one of the comments that has been passed is that the research ideology is both self-limiting and almost didactic.

The process of action learning within a community of peers, however, provides what is felt are some steps towards ensuring its validity. The students themselves will own validation of their research process, through a focus not only on the relevance of the practical, but its improvement using systematic inquiry and reflexivity. By producing a researched and written output, the course members will add to the collection of 'case studies' to which other practitioners and peers can give validity by referencing. Thus a degree of generalization can occur, and this is reinforced locally in the programme through challenge and response within the learning set. Here, set members will not only be provoked to consider the right answers, but also to ask the appropriate questions. A form of critical and reflective dialogue will therefore be developed, not only within the set, but also in the student's organization by examining if change has occurred, and this form of collaboration will generate a powerful validity by the 'clients' of the students' application of their learning.

The learning set itself has a pivotal role to ensure the quality and accuracy of the data collection process, data analysis and the context in which the inquiry is being pursued (McCutcheon and Jung, 1990), and almost becomes what McNiff (1988) has described as a 'validation group' whose task is to 'listen attentively to the ... claim to knowledge, consider the evidence and agree that movement has or has not taken place ... critically assess(ing) the action with the researcher and agree(ing) criteria and examples in action that show the realisation of values through practice' (p.134). This further reinforces the dialogic nature of an action research process, as well as its critical pedagogy (Freire, 1972).

The nature of action research is democratic, emancipatory empowerment of the learner. This concept also caused us to consider the nature of curriculum delivery and management, and to ensure that within the Master's project supervision and supported learning sets the notion of 'facilitation' was a paramount consideration, so that the set advisers (who would work with the sets until the end of the course) become not only a source of practical help, but mediators within the group and of learning processes; and also who would be sensitive to maintaining student autonomy but at the same time encourage socially critical action research by the participants. The strength of the team delivering the programme lay in their different expertise, and the synergy that could occur from the close collaboration of those with research backgrounds and those who had senior and deep knowledge of human resource issues. To ensure support, and in line with the collaborative value of the course delivery, a 'buddy' system of informal mentoring is planned, with each individual in the pair providing an expert resource on which the other could rely.

Through the dialogue created, which is a distinctive strategy, we believe that the learning between teacher and manager – as well as the teaching – is two-way. In the modern organization, managers are teachers and the action learning process is a transformative approach highly suitable for those in the 'learning organization'.

The areas discussed above were only a small number of a much wider set of issues faced in the course design but they were perhaps crucial considerations. The launch of the programme in 1993 provides a valuable opportunity for further research into the social processes involved in work-based professional learning with the link between problem solving and personal development, and the benefits of this form of management development to organizational effectiveness.

BRIDGING THE ACADEMIC/PRACTITIONER DIVIDE

In the 1990s a key theme being addressed in the professions is that of 'continuous professional development' (CPD) including continuing education, and managers and professionals are expected to demonstrate evidence of their CPD activity to achieve fellowship, or to simply retain recognition of their professional competence, which in some cases means the right to practise. While accreditation of the individual's learning should not be an end in itself, practitioners are increasingly aware of higher education's willingness to give recognition for demonstrable learning which takes place beyond the formal environs of classroom-based activity and internal assessment. Action research and action learning processes provide a generic approach to a diverse range of professions for practitioners to obtain professional fellowship at the same time as really improving their own effectiveness in the workplace, as well as making a contribution through critical social research to better understanding of business and professional activity. The approach's collaborative philosophy will also be particularly useful in forging new links and connections between the industry-based practitioner and the university researcher.

REFERENCES

Boddy, D (1984) 'Putting action learning into action', in Mumford, A (ed.) *Insights in Action Learning*, Bradford: MCB University Press.

Boisot, M and Fiol, M (1987) 'Chinese boxes and learning cubes: action learning in a cross-cultural context', *The Journal of Management Development*, 6, 2, 8–18.

Elliott, J (1991) 'A model of professionalism and its implications for teacher education', *British Educational Research Journal*, 17, 4, 309–17.

Freire, P (1972) *Pedagogy of the Oppressed*, Harmondsworth: Penguin.

Halsey, A H (ed) (1972) *Educational Priority Volume 1: Educational priority area problems and policies*, London: HMSO.

Harries, J M (1991, 2nd ed) 'Developing a set adviser', in Pedlar, M (ed), *Action learning in practice*, Aldershot: Gower.

Kemmis, S (1988) 'Action research in retrospect and prospect', in Kemmis, S and McTaggart, R (eds), *The Action Research Reader*, Victoria: Deakin University Press.

Kolb, D A (1984) *Experiential Learning: Experience as the source of learning and development*, Englewood Cliffs, NJ: Prentice-Hall.

Leavitt, H J (1972) *Managerial Psychology* (3rd ed), Chicago: Chicago University Press.

Lewin, K (1952) 'Field theory in social science', in Cartwright, D (ed.) *Selected Theoretical Papers*, London: Tavistock.

McCutcheon, G and Jung, B (1990) 'Alternative perspectives on action research', *Theory into Practice*, 24, 3, 144–51.

McGill, I and Beaty, L (1992) *Action Learning: A practitioner's guide*, London: Kogan Page.

MacNamara, M and Weekes, W H (1982) 'The action learning model of experiential learning for developing managers', *Human Relations*, 35, 10, 879–902.

MacNamara, M, Mayer, M and Arnold, A (1990) 'Management education and the challenge of action learning', *Higher Education*, 19, 419–33.

McNiff, J (1988) *Action Research: Principles and Practice*, London: Routledge.

Mezirow, J (1981) 'A critical theory of adult learning and education', in *Adult Education*, 32, 1, 3–24.

Revans, R W (1971) *Developing Effective Managers*, London: Praeger.

Revans, R W (1976) 'Action learning – a management development programme', *Personnel Review*, 1, 36–44.

Revans, R W (1983) *ABC of Action Learning* (2nd edn), Southall: Chartwell-Bratt.

Schön, D (1983), *The Reflective Practitioner*, London: Temple Smith.

Thorpe, R (1988) 'An MSc by action learning: a management development initiative by higher degree', *Management Education and Development,* 19, 1, 68–78.

Thorpe, R, and Taylor, M (1991) 'Action learning in an academic context', in Pedlar, M (2nd edn), *Action Learning in Practice,* Aldershot: Gower.

Wallace, M (1987) 'A historical review of action research: some implications for the education of teachers in their managerial role', *Journal of Education for Teaching,* 13, 2, 97–115.

Whitehead, J (1989) 'Creating a living educational theory from questions of the kind, "how do I improve my practice"', *Cambridge Journal of Education,* 19, 1, 41–52.

Willmott, H (1994) 'Management education: provocation to a debate', *Management Learning,* 25, 1, 105–36.

Woodcock, C (1991) 'Bridging the gap between academia and industry', *The Guardian,* 11 February, p.31.

Zuber-Skerritt, O (1992) *Professional Development in Higher Education: A theoretical framework for action research,* London: Kogan Page.

Chapter 15

How Students Acquire Research Skills: SHAPING a Degree at Bangor

Della Fazey and John Fazey

INTRODUCTION

In 1978 the introduction of physical education as a BA with Educational Studies was intend to expand the undergraduate numbers in the school of education at UCNW Bangor. Much has changed since then. The school now has a division of health and human performance which runs an undergraduate programme that continues to expand from the base of a single honours degree called Sport, Health and Physical Education (SHAPE). The programme, which will allow students to graduate with single or joint honours degrees in sport science, health promotion or physical education combined with a range of arts, humanities, sciences and social sciences, is probably best seen as an example of how a liberal science education can be offered with minimal resources. The emergence of the current structures and processes and the philosophy which has guided that development has been a 15-year-long example of proactive and reactive planning, of using action research approaches to curriculum development and of the application of simple survival techniques in the academic politics of the 1980s.

This chapter reports some key outcomes of developments in the SHAPE programme which should be generalizable across HE. In particular it seeks to highlight the fundamental principles on which it was built and how progressive change has led us to turn our thinking inside out. The principles continue to develop but the underlying philosophy which guides an ethos of commitment to teaching stems from the recognition of the need to apply the knowledge we have about learning to what we offer students and to what we understand about our own professional and personal development. We want to be able to do what is best, not just talk about it. We want to walk the talk. Of course, because we are pushing our own limits, sometimes we fall on our faces, but then walking is best described as a series of narrowly averted minor catastrophes. If we do not put the next foot forward with sufficient confidence to stay only nearly upright, we do not keep moving forward. The trick has been to learn how to turn the momentum of a recovery into a force for development.

RESEARCH SKILLS: THE PRIMARY GOAL

The successive refinements in undergraduate teaching are predicated on a deliberate decision, taken at the outset, to make what Bangor offered in the world of physical education distinctive. The idea was to fill a niche that even the best were not filling. The strategy was to offer an academic training in the area which would match that given in the better North American institutions at masters degree level. The programme was designed to provide a rigorous introduction to the process of formulating theoretically-driven questions about the world of physical education. Understanding how to do it, at a level of being a competent beginner in using the process of scientific enquiry, was placed at the head of the objectives of the programme, and acquiring techniques or skills was placed at the core of the degree. Becoming well acquainted with the field was maintained as a requirement in line with the traditional HE emphasis on knowledge acquisition.

The important features which have supported sound development towards those objectives seem to derive from the shared commitment to the change of focus made by those responsible for organizing the degree. This change was a move away from the accumulation of a body of knowledge in the sense of knowing answers in as far as they exist, to operating at the edge of what is known and engaging in the development of the relevant theories which explain the known and generate predictions about what is not yet known. It was a conscious move towards fostering a learning goal of being able to ask theoretically valid questions and being able to devise a reliable way of answering them. The other aspect which supported continued development seems to be that, in helping students aspire to personal, theoretical views of the world in which they want to operate, staff have been willing to extend their own understanding of the teaching and learning processes involved. There has been a continuing development of the teachers' theoretical understanding of the learning world especially as it relates to students of HE. A distinct advantage that we have always had is that much of what we focus on as content is also bound up in what we have to learn to do to become competent learners. Of course a precondition of being a competent teacher is to be a competent learner.

Whatever else may have changed, a deliberate effort has been made to keep the primary orientation of the original degree. The research process is still at the centre of what is offered and colours much of what students are expected to do as they learn how to use the process.

THE PROCESS OF ENQUIRY

The primary goal of developing theoretically based views of the world in which we operate translated, in the past, into strategic objectives which superficially look very similar to those laid out for many degree courses developed over the last ten or 15 years. Familiarization with the processes of enquiry, as it is represented in Figure 15.1, was achieved by a series of graded experiences which were designed to progressively shift responsibility from the teacher to the learner. The outcomes (indicated in Figure 15.1) incorporated the behaviours we wanted to see in our graduates. It was at quite an early stage that we recognized practice as one of the prime determinants of what governed how well some students could acquire those behaviours. Practice does not mean to simply repeat. It only counts

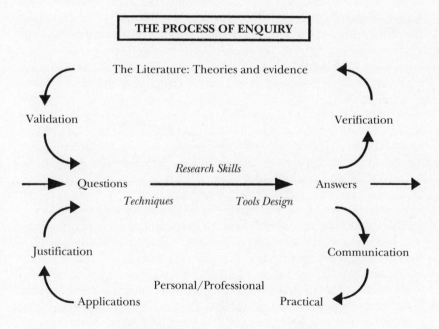

Figure 15.1 *The cyclical process of enquiry*

as practice if it demands invention, creation and progression. Since practice is probably the most crucial variable in learning and the actual amount of practice is a significant factor in determining progress, it seems obvious that the sooner the process starts the better. On day one students have to be expected to begin behaving in the ways you want them to behave at graduation. Of course the criteria for success change as people rehearse and extend their repertoire of skills and techniques as, with practice, they become increasingly skilful. Standards in the final assessment seem to go up from year to year as staff become more proficient at achieving objectives and raise their level of expectations of the outcome.

PRACTICE

The model (Figure 15.2) suggests how practice is achieved by cycling through the process in mini- and macro-cycles several times throughout the whole period of study for the degrees within the division of health and human performance. Some of the mini-cycles inevitably have idiosyncratic as well as collectively determined emphases. This gives practice of stages or phases of the process of enquiry rather than as an holistic experience but the principle still remains. Practice is frequent. It is varied. It is evaluated against criteria that are established at the outset. Feedback from the evaluation is valuable and valued because it also feeds

PRACTICE OF PROCESS

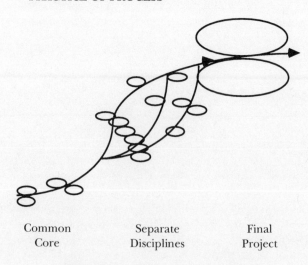

| Common | Separate | Final |
| Core | Disciplines | Project |

Figure 15.2   *Skill acquisition variables*

forward into the next practice and is neither isolated nor necessarily tied to specific summative assessment. We attempt to apply what we teach about to what we teach people to do and to how we teach.

The principles of practice structure are a cornerstone in the area of skill acquisition. Other features of what makes practice effective are also relatively well understood in the developmental, verbal and motor domains. By bringing to bear what we understand about environmental influences and appropriate time-frames we should be able to structure appropriate situation settings for learning. Appropriateness of expected learning and teaching styles is also a central issue of one of the sub-areas in the programme. The progress students make in mastering a range of styles is both determined by and a determinant of what can be used in practice. Practice features which predictably enhance retention, transfer or both in the domains in which we work sit well with the theoretical notions of active rather than passive learning styles and the emergence of perceived competence and self-worth.

Recognizing the dangers of generalizing principles beyond their established validity demands that any attempt to transfer principles from one domain to another has to be viewed as an experiment. Treating teaching as action research as we make such educated guesses fits well with the ethos generated in the programme and brings with it considerable advantages.

AN EXAMPLE

Working in groups: auditing skills

From week one students are encouraged to work in small groups. They are introduced to a systematic way of approaching tasks in a variety of settings.

Second- and third-year students arrange a day in an outdoor environment where a barn acts as a meeting room and physical tasks and problem-solving challenges are devised by the organizers to illustrate the principles of learning from experience.

In class meetings they are introduced to the group skills matrix (Figure 15.3) which allows assessment of the collective skills of group members as a planning tool and a means of identifying areas for potential development for individuals. Those with skills are encouraged to 'teach'. Those without are encouraged to practise. The matrix is simply a sheet ruled out with spaces for names across the top and for the skills necessary to complete the task down the side.

Group members indicate whether they can do things, whether they can

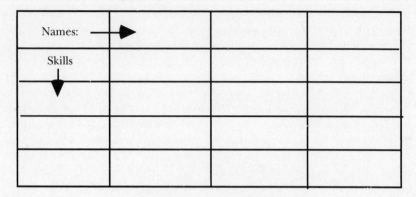

Figure 15.3   *The group skills matrix*

teach others or whether they need to learn from scratch. The skills matrix is emphasized every third week throughout the first term during the 'what makes people skilful' introduction.

The tasks given to groups during the first year culminate in an exercise which demands that they form their own groups to divide up a *class project* which has to be completed in a week, presented to the division in written (word-processed and bound) and verbal formats.

STUDENTS' LEARNING GOALS IN THEORETICALLY-DRIVEN ENQUIRY

Research into the effectiveness of the SHAPE programme

As psychologists we are interested in the response of students to the curriculum with which they are presented and in the changes which occur in them over their time at Bangor. An assumption is that some of the processes that are embedded in the design and implementation of the research-oriented curriculum will stimulate changes in the approaches to study for many students. Observation of student behaviour would support this assumption but it has not, as yet, been verified empirically. A study has just begun which will enable us to describe some of the salient psychological characteristics of our undergraduates and to measure changes over time. This piece of research, in line with the principles underlying the format of the degree programme, will ask questions about the psychological dimensions of SHAPE students which change in response to specific interventions during their undergraduate studies, and inform those involved of the effectiveness of the design and presentation of the programme.

Psychological characteristics

Although there are many dimensions of our lives which might be considered to have a considerable impact on our success in HE, the study which has just begun is considering some of the psychological factors which have been demonstrated as being involved in positive achievement behaviours (Bandura, 1989; Duda and Nicholls, 1992; Van Overwalle and De Metsenaere, 1990). They are:

- learning goals
- perceived academic competence
- motivation to study
- attributional style
- self-regulation.

Several of these factors are considered to overlap or be subordinate to others but often the assumed causal or relational links are unclear or not well-substantiated. Within the SHAPE degree it is anticipated that those students who score positively (eg, high in perceived competence and self-regulation; well-developed learning goals) on these measures will produce high quality research projects and that the changes which occur across the three years of study will relate to the particular experiences within the curriculum. One of the challenges for this research study is the recognition that this is not a one-way relationship, as the autonomous student will change and control the working environment. From a developmental perspective the interaction between the individual and the environment – what Hetherington and Baltes (1988) describe as organismic contextualism – acknowledges the constant dynamic changes which occur within both the person and their environment. The cause-and-effect relationship cannot be denied but the directionality of the relationship is not easily differentiated at any particular point in time.

SELF-REGULATION IN SHAPE

One of the underlying philosophies of those teaching students within the division of health and human performance is that the development of self-regulatory skills leading to autonomous behaviour will greatly enhance the learning process. Observation suggests that the most successful students in recent years have been those who exhibited a desire and ability to organize, initiate and control their own learning within the demands of the degree programme, and the earlier they displayed this characteristic the faster their progress. For instance, within the research focus of the degree, those who are able to work independently while appropriately using resources such as supervisors, postgraduate students and peers, are able to produce a high standard of work in the final experimental project which is the focus of their degree.

HE in a general sense requires more self-regulated learning than do most secondary schools and FE colleges and, for those students who have experienced autonomy before the start of their undergraduate course (often mature students though not all of these or exclusively), this does not present any difficulties. For students whose previous experiences have been externally controlled and directed, self-regulated studies can initially be very difficult. The SHAPE programme aims to encourage the acquisition of self-regulatory skills across the three years of the degree by increasingly requiring students to take control over their learning and encouraging them to initiate opportunities when appropriate. For example, the summatively assessed assignment in year 1 might be about a prescribed topic whereas in year 2 students are required to choose, with guidance, a topic which is of interest to them and in the third year be given a completely free choice, within that subject area, to define their topic. Criteria for achieving successful completion of the assignment must be carefully defined in each case by the tutor, the student and/or the group and opportunities for tutorial discussions made available. Negotiation skills are practised with students increasingly active in the assessment process.

Another example of the way in which the curriculum offers opportunities for self-regulation is in the skills module. Students are required to participate in a specified number of ten-hour units as part of their degree, with all units being practical in nature. The choice ranges from performance-related physical activities, through vocationally-oriented courses to units which address issues such as writing a CV and practising exam techniques. Students may choose to follow as many as they wish and are encouraged to make the decision, where possible, following a personal skills audit which considers strengths, weaknesses and personal goals.

Self-regulation as a skill

Like any other skill, that of self-regulation requires practice and cannot be acquired overnight. Those who arrive at Bangor having had previous opportunities to develop the skill or who are able to develop the skill early in their undergraduate careers, are at an advantage when faced with an independent research project. Deci and Ryan (1985) described self-regulation as a basic human need as well as, '. . . a capacity to choose and to have those choices, rather than reinforcement contingencies, drives or any other forces or pressures, be the determinants of one's actions' (p.38).

Although Deci and Ryan view the human species as being predisposed to strive for self-regulation or determination they also state that the environment can enhance or deter the process of development. Given an innate desire to be in control, there must be appropriate opportunities for people to explore and practise self-regulation in non-threatening situations. During the first term of the first year in SHAPE, students are asked to consider the question, 'What makes people skilful?' Possible answers to this question are investigated by looking at three subject areas (development, learning and information processing), using a variety of learning situations (eg, lectures, library searches, teaching sessions with children, learning a physical skill). No answers to the question are given or accepted as *the* answer and a climate is developed which encourages active participation, sharing of skills and investigation. Students who are attentive to, involved in and openly question the tasks set are reinforced for their behaviour, providing models for others. In the second and third years students are given increasing opportunities to practise their questioning skills alongside the 'knowledge' component of the degree. In one module the 'content' element is explored using experimental experiences to find out what facts are needed to answer the question set and then, by request, the teacher will provide these facts or initiate the discussion which examines the issue. This is a very active learning situation which is unnerving for those students who prefer to be told the facts or who are unsure about their competence in this situation. Careful support of those students is required if they are to continue to develop (Smith, 1993).

GOAL-SETTING

Appropriate goal-setting leads to the recognition of achievement and supports intrinsically-motivated activity in mastery-oriented people. Within the area of sport, health and physical education, students study the literature on goal-setting that explains why goals should be challenging yet achievable, measurable and specific, and accepted by the individual. A prerequisite of goal setting is the ability to assess existing capability – you cannot plan the way forward until you know where you are now. Self-assessment opportunities, which encourage students to recognize their own and others' strengths and weaknesses are integrated into the course using a group skills matrix. This is described in detail elsewhere (Fazey, 1993b) and involves assessing individual skills within a small group and comparing them with a list of skills which are identified as required within the degree. The group members then set goals in relation to existing and target skills and are responsible for supporting each member of the group in achieving the goals set within the group. The responsibility for progress lies with the students and, although opportunities for organizing the group activity are provided initially, the inherent value of the system is recognized, valued and self-sustaining for the majority. There are, inevitably, some students who do not take full advantage of the support of their peers but for those who do, skill acquisition is enhanced and a climate is engendered in which there is a collaborative investment in development. Implicitly involved in the successful outcome of this activity are the self-regulation and intrinsic motivation attributes which have been demonstrated as being closely linked to positive achievement behaviour (see for instance Bandura, 1989; Deci and Ryan, 1985) and students who already display behaviours associated with these attributes provide models for others. If this behaviour is reinforced by significant others (eg, lecturers) then learning will occur.

At the individual level some first-year students are offered the opportunity to use a diary as a tool for personal development (Fazey, 1993a) and a major feature of this procedure is the setting of personal goals which are both proximal and distal. Tutorial support is given to the student to help him/her develop techniques for setting appropriate goals and recording achievement. Most second- and third-year students do not need to continue to use the diary but some choose to do so, while others use alternative methods such as action plans. Discussion of these methods of setting goals takes place with a personal tutor or student adviser.

Within the design of the degree programme, as an explicit aid to self-regulatory skills, all assignments and deadlines are set at the beginning of the term to enable students to organize their time. Any extensions to deadlines must be negotiated a week before the deadline unless an emergency occurs. The importance of ownership of goals is underlined by many authors (see for instance Locke and Latham, 1985) and is an inherent part of the development and maintenance of autonomy.

The extent to which the goals which we, as teachers, have set for the students become personal goals will be an interesting aspect of the study which has just begun. Volet and Chalmers (1992) suggest that learning goals gradually unfold during development with the most naive being an intention to 'remember key features of theories and the area of study' and the most highly developed in the hierarchy being to 'construct your own theoretical perspective of the area studied'. If the declared aim of the SHAPE degree is to enable students to become competent researchers, with an ability to be creative, then the majority of students should, at some point in their undergraduate career, adopt learning goals commensurate with those of the teachers. As Volet and Chalmers point out, the internalization of goals at the 'deeper' end of the process can only occur if the individual recognizes that this level of learning exists. The environment must provide opportunities and models if students are to attain the declared objective of the SHAPE programme which is to develop a personal, theoretical view of the areas of study.

PERCEIVED COMPETENCE

Nicholls (1984) argued that people will seek situations in which they can demonstrate competence and avoid those in which they feel they are likely to appear incompetent. The development of a perception of academic competence involves the interaction of many variables including previous experience and attributional style but it is important to recognize that an individual's perception of competence is a powerful mediator of behaviour (eg, Bandura, 1989; Eshel and Kerman, 1991; Harter, 1989). Beginning undergraduates present a challenge to teaching staff who must enable their students to acquire appropriate perceptions of their abilities in relation to the task demands (Fazey, 1993a). Within the SHAPE degree such activities as the personal development diary and group skills matrix already described encourage students to recognize strengths and tackle deficits overtly. The evaluation of competence within the research ethos of the degree has to be an ongoing process with developmentally appropriate tasks set to enable students to practise skills and challenge themselves to improve.

Making verbal presentations to peers is viewed as part of the research process and, from the start of their degree, students are presented with opportunities to verbally present information informally within and between small groups, as individuals to a small group in a summatively-assessed situation and finally in an open-audience research proposal. The learning process thus creates a sense of adequate competence to meet the increasing demands of the task. This is, of course, not a new idea. The sound pedagogical principle of setting achievable, challenging tasks is an inherent part of good teaching, though some teachers in HE seem to be unaware of the importance of students' perceptions of their abilities and focus only on actual competence.

THE TRANSITION

In the early stages of implementing the programme the chosen focus was on practising the research skills. Techniques, tools and principles of design were offered as things to learn about and things to learn to do. In the middle years of development we became increasingly aware of the need to make explicit the personal skills which underpin learning how to research. A pattern of supported learning evolved, making self-regulatory skills increasingly explicit. The programme carried the banner as Bangor moved into the Enterprise in Higher Education operation and provided a lead for departments wishing to associate with the capability in HE movement. At about that time (1988/9) we recognized the need for a more radical change in our perspective. We had moved from the initial position of developing specific skills for a specific target outcome to one in which the central vehicle for education we offered remained research but it was being carried along by developing personal skills. The final move was to put the acquisition of personal skills at the core of what we do and make it the engine which powers the vehicle. Levels of commitment to this principle vary amongst those involved in teaching the programme but sufficient are committed to make the necessary impact. The development of staff is contingent upon the learning environment just as it is for students, and supportive opportunities have to be consistently offered. Given the pressures of research selectivity exercises and teaching quality assessment which inevitably draw everyone back to the safe ground of the tried and tested, providing the support and the motivation is increasingly difficult.

We have developed our own theoretical perspective of learning in HE. It is process-oriented and draws heavily on the theories of development, learning and performance that we teach. We trust that, in exposing our students to a process which is contrived to apply the best of what can be predicted to support effective learning, we offer a model which they can follow. We also trust that it is a model which is both eclectic and rigorous in demonstrating the multi-disciplinary approach required to understand and explain what happens as we become more skilful.

We believe that students need models rather than critics, for they cannot be perfect and neither can we, but we also know that we do not have to be bad to get better.

REFERENCES

Bandura, A (1989) 'Perceived self-efficacy in the exercise of personal agency', *The Psychologist*, 10, 411–24.

Deci, E L and Ryan, R M (1985) *Intrinsic Motivation and Self-Determination in Human Behaviour*, New York: Plenum.

Duda, J L and Nicholls, J G (1992) 'Dimensions of achievement motivation in schoolwork and sport', *Journal of Educational Psychology*, 84, 1–10.

Eshel, Y and Kerman, J (1991) 'Academic self-concept, accuracy of perceived ability and academic attainment', *British Journal of Educational Psychology*, 61, 2, 187–96.

Fazey, D M A (1993a) '"They can because they think they can": the role of perceived competence in learning', paper presented at the Innovations in Teaching Conference, University of Wales, Bangor, Gwynedd, Wales.

Fazey, D M A (1993b) 'Self-assessment as a generic skills for enterprising students: the learning process. Assessment and evaluation in higher education'.

Fazey J A (1989) 'Negotiating criteria for assessment', Using Learning Contracts in Higher Education Conference, Higher Education for Capability, RSA, London.

Harter, S (1989)' Causes, correlates and the functional role of global self-worth: a life-span perspective', in Kolligan, J and Sternberg R (eds), *Perception of Competence and Incompetence Across the Life-Span*, New Haven, CT: Yale University Press.

Hetherington, M and Baltes, P (1988) 'Child psychology and life-span development', in Hetherington, E M, Lerner, R M and Perlmutter, M (eds), *Child Development in Life-Span Perspective*, London: Lawrence Erlbaum.

Locke, E A and Latham, G P (1985) 'The application of goal-setting to sports', *Journal of Sports Psychology*, 7, 205–22.

Nicholls, J G (1984) 'Striving to demonstrate and develop ability: a theory of achievement motivation', in Nicholls, J G (ed.) *Advances in Motivation and Achievement: The development of achievement motivation (Vol. 3)*, Greenwich, CT: JAI Press.

Smith, P J (1993) 'Developing research skills in undergraduates', poster presented at the Innovations in Teaching and Learning Conference, EHE Unit, University of Wales, Bangor, Gwynedd, Wales.

Van Overwalle, F and De Metsenaere, M (1990) 'The effects of attribution-based intervention and study strategy training on academic achievement in college freshmen', *British Journal of Educational Psychology*, 60, 299–311.

Volet, S E and Chalmers, D (1992) 'Investigation of qualitative differences in university students' learning goals, based on an unfolding model of stage development', *British Journal of Educational Psychology*, 62, 17–34.

Chapter 16

Research Learning on the Essex MBA

Sean McCartney and Reva Berman Brown

INTRODUCTION

The debate on teaching and research in higher education tends to start from the viewpoint that they are separate activities, even if mutually dependent. One school of thought is that good teaching is enhanced by the conducting of research by the teachers, or at any rate in the institution. Another view is that in a research institution, teaching is inevitably seen as a less worthy activity. From this perspective, the best teaching would take place in dedicated institutions by dedicated teachers who see their mission as teaching. One view of the 'binary divide' which existed in higher education in the UK until recently was that universities had a mission to research, while polytechnics had a mission to teach. While differing views have been put forward as to the quality of teaching in the two types of institutions, there has been little challenge to the teaching/research dichotomy.

This chapter reviews the teaching/learning strategy on the part-time MBA at Essex and uses the experience to provide such a challenge. The Essex MBA teaches by means of research learning: students identify areas of interest/concern to themselves and their organizations and conduct research into them. That is to say, the teaching method (of the staff) is research (by the student). Teaching and research are indivisible.

TEACHING AND RESEARCH

In his contribution to a recent compendium of essays on enhancing the learning process (1992), Malcolm Frazer, chief executive of the Higher Education Quality Council, agrees with the traditional view that good teaching must be underpinned by research. He lists five characteristics of a 'quality teacher' in rank order, the first being, 'Up-to-date professional knowledge, skills and competence in the subject. This is the sine qua non for every teacher' (p.57). He goes on to comment (p.56) that this characteristic,

...makes it essential for teachers in higher education to have time and resources to be engaged in research or some other form of professional or scholarly activity. The effort and time to be devoted to such activity will vary from subject to subject and individual to individual but should never be zero. Research activity is part of preparing for teaching.

Later, he comments (p.59) that,

Traditionally, universities have had three functions: (1) to generate, (2) to safeguard, and (3) to transmit knowledge. Not all institutions in higher education now place functions (1) and (2) high in their missions, but nevertheless their teachers must be active in research if teaching, function (3), is to be effective.

We see problems with this rationale for research activity. Take the first quotation. Leaving aside the meaning of 'skills and competence in the subject', we can probably all agree on the need for teachers to be up-to-date. The problem arises in the deduction made from this. Here, we want to stress that we are referring in particular to professional/vocational areas. (The authors are teachers/researchers in accounting and management, respectively). It does not at all follow that a teacher keeping up-to-date with such a subject is necessarily engaged in research, as that word is usually understood. After all, the need to be up-to-date applies just as much to practitioners as to teachers – perhaps even more so. Naturally, the literature being read by the practitioner and the academic will differ to a greater or lesser extent, but that is a different issue. Yet no one would suggest that an accountant, for example, must engage in '...research or some other form of professional or scholarly activity' unless keeping abreast of current technical developments, admittedly an arduous and time-consuming task, be defined as such. And if this falls under the heading of '...other...activity', then it is a distinct activity from research, and should not be confused with it. Similarly, a teacher of accounting must keep up-to-date with the literature in the areas he or she is teaching, but this is not in itself research. We can go further: much academic research is so specialized, not to say esoteric, that its relationship with the teaching of the researcher, in terms of subject matter, can be tangential or even non-existent. For example, one of the authors of this chapter is currently engaged in research into 'Management letters'. These are letters sent by company auditors to the management of auditee companies making recommendations on improving company procedures, etc. He also teaches on the sole auditing course offered by the University of Essex, which is available as an option to final year undergraduates.

Management letters are covered, among other topics, in a single session of a ten-week one-term course, ie only a small portion of 10 per cent of the subject matter of the entire course. It is not immediately obvious how this research constitutes 'part of preparing for teaching'. One might with more justice argue first, that, being such a small part of the course, it is only there as a form of self-indulgence on the part of the teacher, and second, that the research is actually a diversion from (preparing for) teaching, which might have deleterious effects on the latter's quality.

Many people do, in fact, take this view. For example, Sir Christopher Ball, former chairman of the National Advisory Board for Higher Education in England (the NAB as it was known) argues along these lines. Making a distinction between 'fundamental research', 'contract research', and 'scholarship and advanced study', Ball argues that while the third category is essential for all teachers in higher education, fundamental research is not. The artificial tying of fundamental research to teaching is inhibiting both the expansion of higher education (because of the additional cost of the comcomitant research effort) and the development of a rational policy on the public funding of fundamental research (Ball, 1992). The recent changes in the way the HEFC allocates research funds are in accord with this line of argument.

We reiterate Frazer's argument as follows:

Teachers need to keep up-to-date in their subjects.
This requires '. . . professional or scholarly activity'
This comes under the same heading as research.
Thus, '. . . teachers (in universities) must be active in
research, if teaching is to be effective'.

Frazer has not provided a rationale for his statement that research is necessary to underpin teaching. The aim of this chapter is to provide such a rationale, based on recent research into the nature of teaching and learning, and drawing on the experience of the MBA programme delivered at the University of Essex. A major theme of recent literature has been the 'debunking' of what might be called the 'traditional' approach to classroom teaching, which is seen as having too great an emphasis on the students' ability to acquire and record knowledge (Stephenson and Weil, 1992). A number of writers have developed and promoted the concept of 'deep learning' as distinct from the 'surface learning' inculcated by traditional methods (for example, Biggs, 1989; Boud and Felletti, 1991; Gibbs, 1992; Ramsden, 1988). This body of theory was drawn on during the design of the MBA at the University of Essex, of which the authors are currently co-directors.

The order of the chapter is as follows: first, it outlines the rationale of the MBA at the University of Essex, and shows how, in practice, the dichotomy between learning and research can be overcome, with a new term 'research learning' being used to describe the process. It then looks at the concept of deep learning, describing the theory by which the Essex MBA programme was guided. It shows that this concept, which in the last few years has been central to attempts to improve the student learning experience in British higher education, can be seen as a partial form of research learning, a new education process which has been successful insofar as, and precisely because, it attempts to make that pedagogical experience more closely resemble research. Problem-based learning is discussed and the Essex MBA's version of this is introduced. The chapter then endeavours to draw out some general lessons on the relationship between teaching and research in higher education. Finally, it sets out the structure of the part-time MBA at the University of Essex.

RATIONALE OF THE PROGRAMME

In designing the MBA, a deliberate decision was made to exclude exams. Formal assessment is purely on the basis of tutor assessment. The student is expected to submit eight term papers (one in the area covered by each module) and two dissertations (at the end of each of the two academic years over which the programme extends). The term papers and dissertations are blind double-marked, and the final mark is correlated by discussion between the markers. The piece of work is then sent to an external examiner for validation. There is no requirement that the students demonstrate that they have absorbed every (or any particular) aspect of a corpus of knowledge presented in a module.

Research learning

From the point of view of the student, while attendance at formal classes is expected, the bulk of the time and effort which students spend on the MBA is devoted to the preparation of their term papers and dissertations, and it is through this process that most learning takes place. Moreover, what is learned is driven by the needs of the paper which the student is preparing. Existing knowledge is assimilated ('A review of the literature on motivation') as a consequence of the desire to acquire new knowledge ('How XYZ Ltd motivates it employees'). In short, what the students are actually engaged in is research.

Let us note two obvious characteristics of the course:

- The students have a large measure of control over what they learn. This is partially true of even the formal classes, and almost entirely true of their papers.

- The students are generating knowledge, as well as acquiring it. (The usefulness of this knowledge is a different question.) We can point out, however, that the traditional view of doctoral study is that the purpose of it is not so much to generate new knowledge, though this may happen, but to enable the student to learn how to research.

DEEP AND SURFACE LEARNING

Studies have identified a number of concepts of learning, ranging from the most superficial to the most sophisticated, as seen by the learner. A number of writers, for example Gibbs (1992), have developed a distinction between 'deep learning' and 'surface learning'. In deep learning, the intention is to understand, and the student maintains the structure of the task; in surface learning, the intention is only to complete the task requirements, and the student distorts the structure of the task (Ramsden, 1992, p.46). We will not attempt to rehearse these ideas here, except to summarize below the contrasting features of the two modes of learning:

Deep Approach to Learning

1. The focus is on 'what is signified', eg the concepts applicable to solving the problem.

2. Relates previous knowledge to new knowledge.

3. Relates knowledge from different courses.

4. Relates theoretical ideas to everyday experience.

5. Relates and distinguishes evidence and argument.

6. Organizes and structures content into a coherent whole.

7. The emphasis is internal and the impulse to learn comes from within the student.

Surface Approach to Learning

1. The focus is on the 'signs', for example, the words and sentences of the text, or the formulae needed to solve the problem.

2. The focus is on unrelated parts of the task.

3. Information for assessment is simply memorized.

4. Facts and concepts are associated unreflectively.

5. Principles are not distinguished from examples.

6. The task is treated as an external imposition.

7. The emphasis is external and the impulse to learn comes from the demands of assessment.

(Ramsden, 1992)

Accepting the above as a theoretical framework, many contributions and much of the discussion on the question of improving student learning address themselves to the question of shifting student learning experience away from surface to deep learning by, for example, appropriate course design. We claim that the characteristics of deep learning are all characteristics of the Essex MBA. The design of the course simply excludes a surface approach.

It is also striking that the characteristics of deep learning listed above are (or should be) typical of research generally. In other words, the deep learning characteristics of the MBA course are brought into being because the students are being compelled to learn by means of research. Changing the student experience in a way that inculcates deep learning is tantamount to making it more like research, with one obvious difference: the literature on deep learning assumes that the knowledge the student is acquiring is already in existence, that he or she is not engaged in generating new knowledge. We can see this more clearly by looking at the question of deep learning strategies. The Essex MBA uses all these strategies, to a greater or lesser extent, but the method used most closely approaches what is called problem-based learning.

Problem-based learning

The generally-accepted meaning of problem-based learning (PBL) is that it involves learning through tackling relevant problems. This is not the same as learning how to solve problems. Indeed, the problem on which the proposed learning is based may not be solvable because the aim of this method is for the student to learn rather than to achieve a problem-solution. It is through their confrontation with the problem that students discover what it is that they need to learn about, and they then proceed to learn what is necessary in order to tackle the problem. Put simplistically, in PBL, students start with problems and find out what they need to know (usually in teams) to make progress with that problem. In this sense, there is no 'teaching'. Gibbs (1992, p.14) provides the main features of problem-based learning:

1.   The problems presented are relevant. In professional courses such as engineering or management, it is possible to give students real-world problems to tackle. These problems are carefully designed to involve all the important parts of the syllabus or teaching programme. The Harvard Business School case studies are examples of this approach and have been adopted and emulated wherever management is taught.

2.   A 'need to know' is created. Motivation is generated because the students' learning is governed by what is necessary for them to be able to tackle the problem.

3.   Knowledge is integrated. The selected real-world problems are interdisciplinary and strategic or large-scale. Students are required to create combinations of knowledge/subject areas in order to deal with the problem.

4.   There is student interaction. Problem-based learning is designed in such a way as to require students to work in co-operative groups, sharing their ideas, dividing up the learning and briefing each other as they proceed towards the problem-solution.

The Essex MBA is thus not strictly one of classical problem-based learning. While it contains the four features outlined above, there are a number of differences.

The basic point about the problems on the majority of PBL programmes is that these have been previously and carefully selected in order to provide material for students to cover the syllabus/topic in a manner conducive to self-learning. The Essex MBA does not have a fixed syllabus. The problem-based approach, often in the form of real-world case studies, is used during the teaching sessions, but it is obvious to students that these are exemplars, providing the kind of problems that managers are confronted with so that they can make connections between theory and practice.

The requirement is that problems covered by the term papers and dissertations are generated by the students themselves. There is thus no opportunity on the part of the MBA tutors to design or select problems for the students to consider in their term papers. Motivation is highly focused expressly because the problems selected by the students are practically relevant to them and their organizations. They see the problem which they research and write about as relevant both to their studies and their careers. There is no need to simulate real-world problems for examination in the term papers and dissertations because these deal with actual real-world problems.

While the PBL which takes place during the teaching sessions will require cooperative working and idea-sharing, the term papers and dissertations are individual pieces of work, particular to the student who has chosen the problem for personal and professional reasons. While the students discuss these during the teaching sessions and in their learning groups, accepting peer-group guidance, they are on their own in producing the piece of written work.

THE RELATIONSHIP BETWEEN TEACHING AND RESEARCH

The principal learning vehicles on the Essex MBA are the term papers and dissertations, on which most of the students' energy is expended. Each student therefore has a unique learning experience, based on issues/problems in their own organizations, to which their particular knowledge base can be applied, and on which they are required to reflect in each paper. A further point is that since assessment is based entirely on the papers and dissertations, there is no divorce between the learning experience and the assessment of that experience. The deliberate exclusion of exams from the assessment system removes the likelihood of fostering a surface learning approach.

Our contention is that the deep learning characteristics of the Essex MBA programme are a product of what we have termed 'research learning'. Indeed, we think we can go further and generalize this statement. Where changes have been made by teachers in higher education to the courses they deliver, in an attempt to promote deep learning in line with the ideas being expressed above, what they have actually done is to make those courses (typically undergraduate courses), more like research.

We can visualize learning/research activity as having three key variables:

- autonomy of content: the extent to which the student controls *what* he or she learns;

- autonomy of learning method: the extent to which the student controls *how* he or she learns;

- Generation of new knowledge: the extent to which the student is *generating new knowledge,* as distinct from simply assimilating existing knowledge.

In the 'traditional' mode of teaching that which is to be learned, tutors are assumed to possess the knowledge, which is transmitted to the students, who have no control over what it is they are required to learn or how they learn it. Thus both types of student autonomy listed above are non-existent, and the knowledge being assimilated (or not, as is too often the case) is already known. At the other extreme, in some academic research, both types of autonomy are almost total, and the knowledge being generated is new. Other learning experiences involve these variables in various combinations. Deep learning can be seen in this model as increasing the autonomy in the first two variables. It still assumes, however, that there is a defined body of knowledge which is possessed by the tutors, and which is to be absorbed by the student. The concentration is on improving the effectiveness of this process of absorption.

We think our experience enables us to challenge this underlying assumption. It seems that our MBA has been successful in developing our students' potential to become better managers. They may not know very much in the factual sense, but they understand fully what it is they know. More importantly, they know how to discover and learn that which they do not know, as and when it is relevant to them. As a result, by the end of the programme, they may not *know* anything in particular, to any depth, or in any detail, but they have *learned* a great deal.

We think this has general relevance to higher education, notwithstanding the unusual features of a part-time MBA: the maturity of the students, the fact that the course is part-time, the obvious ability of the students to use their organizations as the subject for their papers. In other areas of higher education too, the knowledge that the student acquires is less important than learning how to learn. Perhaps we need to concentrate less on the *what,* and more on the *how* and *why* of knowledge.

One student who is also a student of Zen Buddhism, touched on this issue in one of his reflections: 'One of the central themes of Zen Buddhism is the impossibility of teaching enlightenment: the master, instead, having to guide the pupil into self-realisation' (second-year dissertation). This would not be a bad dictum for us as teachers.

THE STRUCTURE OF THE ESSEX MBA

Learning on the two-year programme involves eight thematic 'modules', as we have termed them, and two dissertations, one in each year. In year 1 the modules are Managing People, Financial Information, the External

Environment, and Strategy. In year 2 the modules are Managing Corporate Finance, Information Systems, Decision-Making, and Organizational Development.

Two modules are undertaken in each term, and the summer term is devoted to the dissertation. An obvious feature of this structure is the abolition of the core-course/elective-course divide; there is no fixed core syllabus which is compulsory and which is examined before students can 'progress' to electives. In a sense, all the modules are composed of/contain elements which are available as 'electives'.

A great deal of discussion has taken place in the quarter century since the introduction of business schools in the UK about where the degree should fit along the generalist/specialist continuum and the topic/technique divide. A great many students enrol on an MBA expecting to be taught discrete subjects (marketing, operations management, international business) which will be built up like a jigsaw puzzle into a large picture. They also expect to receive practical know-how (the tools and techniques of management) as well as the more theoretical know-about. As a result, MBA courses tend to be composed of core subjects and electives, and knowledge is formally examined: students are explicitly told that the thematic Essex MBA does not satisfy this expectation.

Delivery

The programme lasts two academic years, with students attending one session (afternoon and evening) each week. One thematic area is covered in each of the two class-periods in the Autumn term and there are a further two modules in the Spring term. The modules are thematic, rather than subject- or function-based. In the module 'Managing the external environment' for instance, topics will include marketing, business ethics, international business, theories about how the external environment impinges on organizations and the effects that organizations may have on their environment. The content of a module is relatively flexible in that students may ask for an area to be included, or ask for one to be excluded, and this request is complied with if it seems educationally sensible. The MBA team try to provide them with what they need/want to learn about. At the end of each module, the students must submit a 4,000-word paper demonstrating the application to their own organizations of some of the ideas discussed in the classes. They are required to select the topic they wish to write about: the element of self-selection is an important part of the deep learning experience. Considerable emphasis is placed on discussion of their ideas for papers by the students with the tutors and, more importantly, with each other.

This leads to written proposals created in the second half of the term and handed in for confirmation of feasibility by the appropriate tutor. At the end of the term, a class will be devoted to group discussion of the individual projects: students come to the meeting with their problems (and successes) and can give assistance to others.

The resulting term paper must be submitted by the beginning of the following term for assessment. It is returned to the students by the fifth week of the term, with a grade and written narrative feedback. It should be emphasized that papers are expected to display understanding of theory and familiarity with the literature in the area chosen by the student. The selected area may, however, have formed a small part of the module, and students are not expected to demonstrate any learning beyond what is relevant to their paper. A course text is recommended for each module, which students are required to read. What we expect from students is that they attend classes and participate in discussion, but the subject-based knowledge acquired is probably sketchy, and is not formally assessed. Thus students do not need to know, and are not expected to know, very much about large areas of the notional 'syllabus'. For example, in the module 'Managing people', a student may submit a term paper on one of the theoretical areas, say motivation, in the student's own organization. He or she will be expected, amongst other things, to demonstrate familiarity with the relevant literature on motivation, but may well have chosen to relegate knowing about say, leadership, to reading a chapter in the course text, and attending a class where the concept was presented.

In the Summer Term, the students continue to attend, although there are no formal classes. They meet together informally and with their tutors if they choose to do so, or use the library facilities and develop their end-of-year dissertation (8,000 words in year 1, submitted at the end of the summer term; 15,000 words in year 2, submitted at the beginning of September). At the end of each paper/dissertation, the students are required to articulate, in an appendix, the meaning which the learning experience involved in producing the paper has had for them.

At the beginning of the course, the students are encouraged to form learning groups, which meet informally at times and places of their own choice. The groups form an important part of the course in that it is there that students are able to support and help each other. These learning groups are autonomous, self-selected and sometimes very fluid. There is no input from the tutors, nor any requirement from us that students should monitor and present to us what they do when they meet. They find these groups very effective in providing meaning and direction for their studies; in many of the term papers, acknowledgements include expressions of thanks, for example:

My colleagues in my learning group provided invaluable advice on the format of the study and provided very welcome moral support during moments of high anxiety (first-year term paper).

We make it clear to students what they are required to do, when undertaking their written, assessed work, and the standard they are to aim for in two main ways:

1. The module outline lists what will be looked for in the term paper, eg a strategic or organizational level of 'problem'. An example of the assessment guidelines is:

   The course is assessed by means of a 4,000 word term paper, which is to be handed in on the first Thursday of the summer term. You are to select at least one major concept from the module and explain and explore an aspect of work behaviour with which you are familiar or with which you wish to become familiar, taken from your own work situation. The selection of the assignment is at your discretion. Approval by the course tutor, of the suitability of the project, should be obtained by means of the submission of an abstract before work on the term paper is begun.

2. The course participants are provided with a copy of the pro forma which will be used to assess their work, with the aspects looked for listed. For example,

   Evidence that the relevant literature has been read and evaluated critically.
   Evidence of the integration of theory and practice in a work situation.
   Clarity of presentation of the problem and its analysis.
   Relevance of the conclusions reached/findings to the aims and process of the paper.
   General comments.

REFERENCES

Ball, C (1992) 'Teaching and research', in Wiston, T and Geiger, R (eds) *Research and Higher Education*, SRHE and OU Press.

Biggs, J B (1989) 'Approaches to the enhancement of tertiary teaching', *Higher Education Research and Development*, 8, 7, 7–25.

Boud D and Felletti, G (1991) *The Challenge of Problem-Based Learning*, Beckenham: Croom Helm.

Frazer, M (1992) 'Promoting learning', in Barnett, R (ed.) *Learning to Effect*, Buckingham: The Society for Research into Higher Education/Open University Press.

Gibbs, G (1992) *Improving the Quality of Student Learning*, Bristol: Technical and Educational Services.

Ramsden, P (1988) 'Studying learning: improving teaching', in Ramsden, P (ed.) *Improving Learning: New perspectives*, London: Kogan Page.

Ramsden, P (1992) *Learning to Teach in Higher Education*, London: Routledge.

Stephenson, J and Weil, S (eds) (1992) *Quality in Learning: A capability approach in higher education*, London: Kogan Page.

Chapter 17

Towards Empowering Undergraduate Students as Action Researchers into Student Learning

Tom Wengraf

INTRODUCTION: WHO SHALL DO ACTION RESEARCH?

According to Zuber-Skerritt (1991, p.1),

> action research ... may be defined as collaborative, critical inquiry by the academics themselves (rather than expert educational researchers) into their own teaching practice, into problems of student learning and into curriculum problems. It is professional development through academic course development, group reflection, action, evaluation and improved practice.

In this chapter, I argue that this definition is unnecessarily restrictive: that 'collaborative critical inquiry' can be undertaken by undergraduate students themselves (rather than by expert educational researchers or by expert academic staff or postgraduates on professional courses). I argue that undergraduate students can undertake such inquiry into what might be reformulated as 'their own *learning practice* and into the problems of *teachers teaching*'.

I argue that undergraduate students are professional learners who need *institutionalized* support from academic staff to enable them to be 'professionally reflective' (Schön, 1987) about their practice as students. They need this support from academic staff in the support of 'institutionalized self-research' precisely to the extent that worsening SSRs (staff:student ratios) and mass modularization mean that staff's *informal* grasp of the conditions of student learning can no longer be relied on to substitute for student self-knowledge achieved through institutionally-supported and required collective self-research. One way of doing this is to *institutionalize undergraduate student action research as part of ordinary coursework*.

In this chapter, I first give an example of what could be characterized as a start in this direction, and describe how it evolved. I give an example of the report material, then identify what I take to be the distinguishing features which enabled the project to be reasonably successful. I then conclude with a brief discussion of where, in a typical university or college, similar activities could be developed and the uses to which it could be put, and end with some questions.

FIRST-YEAR STUDENT SELF-RESEARCH AT MIDDLESEX – THE INITIAL PROJECT

Aims and design

Students on a human sciences research methods module at Middlesex in 1991–2 were asked in their second semester to do semi-structured interviews for a coursework report. At the time, roughly one-half of the undergraduate programmes at Middlesex had been 'modularized' and 'semesterized': for full-time students, three modules in each semester, two semesters per year. The topic of the report had to be, 'What could be done to improve module X?' The students had a free choice of module and of informants, subject to the restriction that the informants should ideally be two other students and a tutor from the module. They then had to produce their coursework report to a given format.

What were my original aims in designing this piece of coursework?

- To deliver a coded message to the students: your reflection on student experience and suggestions for improvement are important and worthy of study and reporting in line with the Kolb learning cycle.

- To send a clear message to the students as human-science researchers: if you cannot apply the concepts and methods you are learning to your own experiences, then you have not yet learned anything you have learned to use.

- To motivate both interviewers and interviewees for their first exercise in semi-structured interviewing. This is a research method in the human sciences which can typically foster the discovery of subject-centred perspectives. I thought that the topic, 'What could be done to improve module X?' would be of great relevance to first-year students and to the staff with whom they came in contact.

- To motivate me as their tutor to work through their material properly and give them good feedback by choosing a subject of sufficient interest to me as a practising tutor.

How did the initial project develop?

The student researchers were in the second semester of their first year. In respect of interviewing method, they were given about 12 hours (lecture plus workshop training) before going out to do their interviews. They were given a broad interviewing brief. They had freedom to design a question-schedule for their interviews, which might identify 'improvement areas' in advance or might leave the definition of 'improvement areas' to the interviewees. Semi-structured interviews typically operate with relatively open-ended questions, and this was important to the success of the project.

For their coursework assessment, they had to produce a 5,000-word report in four specified sections:

1. In an introduction, they were asked to describe and justify choice of informants and give the question-schedule(s) for the interviews.

2. In the next section, they were asked to provide a transcript of one of the three interviews they undertook, being free to choose either a staff or a student interview for this purpose.

3. The main section which followed was that of 'Interpretation', where they were asked to describe (using chunky quotations), compare and evaluate the results of all three interviews.

4. A final section required them to reflect upon and evaluate the project process as a whole, including the writing-up of their report.

Outcome

In all, some 25 staff and 122 fellow students were interviewed for 10–30 minutes each. Some 49 reports were produced and assessed.

Virtually all the students became very committed to their 'What can be done to improve module X?' activity and put a great amount of energy into doing the research and writing-up the reports. Not only were they more motivated to do the interviews and reports well, they produced much more interesting data of a higher quality than I had anticipated.This method of student-designed and student-conducted semi-structured interviews provided a much deeper vein of feedback about the experience of the curriculum than the more frequently found standard multiple-choice survey questionnaire.

Given the deliberate focus on problems to be remedied and my conscious decision not to specify any system of random sampling, the results did not provide an overall evaluation of first-year modules. What the students did was to illuminate curriculum questions by identifying student perceptions of what students and staff experienced as bad or confusing practice. Similarly, I understand, at the former Birmingham Polytechnic, it was focus groups composed of students who decided each year what the themes should be for the 'student satisfaction survey' that year. What themes students select, what questions they think are most appropriate – these are all themselves data for staff reflection and understanding.

It should not be thought that the students at this level can achieve 'objectivity' and that their recommendations about improvement can be simply acted upon. Very often, the contrast between the transcript and the interpretation supposedly based on it enabled me to identify the student's 'pedagogic ideology' by discovering how they systematically misinterpreted their own data.

FIRST-YEAR STUDENT SELF-RESEARCH AT MIDDLESEX – THE META-ANALYSIS PROJECT

The students produced much better and more interesting data than I expected. Consequently, in addition to the value of the student reports in themselves, standing alone, it was possible, due to the structure of the 49 individual reports, to envisage writing a second-tier meta-analysis (Noblit and Hare, 1988). I do not mean simply summarizing or generalizing their accounts (as one might summarize the results of 49 questionnaires) but rather re-evaluating the meaning of each student report in the light of information they revealed, within each report and together as a whole body of reports, about issues, ideologies, perspectives and perceptions.

'Triangulation' was made easier by two features: one, that each report contained some information from three informants, sifted by a fourth, together with one interview transcript with one of the informants; two, that, though just over one-half of the modules had only one report written about them, seven of the modules had between two and ten student reports written about them. In addition, most of the issues raised were common to many of the modules.

I should stress that, originally, I had no intention of producing a detailed report of my own on the basis of their reports. It was the quality of the work they produced that made me feel that it would be a shame if the material were not brought together and used to inform discussion in the university as a whole.

My meta-analysis was written for circulation primarily to university teachers. It therefore was straightforwardly written to illustrate for teaching staff:

1. a range and pattern of *aspects that were significant* to the student researchers, and to a lesser extent the staff and student interviewees,

2. a range and pattern of responses to those aspects by the staff and student interviewees.

In particular, my eventual meta-report with its large proportion of direct quotes from students and staff talking to students provides a less-censored source of feedback on student's perceptions than is normally available to staff.

Because the researchers are fellow students – typically fellow students on the same module – the interviews with fellow students are likely to be less stilted and more realistic than any conducted by 'outside' researchers. As a clarification of student perspectives, ideology, interpretations and misinterpretations, the method yields a rich pattern of information.

SAMPLE OF THE REPORTING

A flavour of the original student reports and the way in which I used them in my meta-report is suggested by the following extract. It deals with questions of 'obscurity of aims and module design' and its relationship to at least one staff pedagogic ideology:

● Obscurity about educational aims may be **at the level of the module as a whole**:

> 'XX 100 was never a coherent enterprise and as far as I could see never in fact had any coherent aims either … it suggested of course that its main subject was going to be [theme] and it attempted to deal with that as if it had some coherence, but in fact, um, no aims in fact were clearly stated in that, and for the life of me, I think, looking back on it, I can't remember an aim to it at all.'

● Obscurity about educational aims and intended outcomes, the criteria of adequacy that staff and students need to share, may also be **at the level of a given week's work**:

> 'And I'd ask him, I mean when we used to ask him about what the class was about, he'd always turn the question round and send it back to you. I mean, that's useful in some respects because we're not taking his word for everything, we're actually thinking about our own ideas. "I think it's about such and such, this is what I got out of it, this is what I didn't get out of it". It would have been useful if he'd actually told us why he set the exercise. Not necessarily what he'd hoped we would gain from it, yeah.… He

must have done it for specific reasons. I think he didn't do it just to fill in time. I hope he had a specific reason.'

'He wasn't just following a formula, do you think?'

No, I think that most of the time he ... I don't know. Perhaps he was ...'.

Another student, asked about the aims of the tutor taking a particular seminar group, remarked:

'... He just sits there behind you, there's no presence.... God knows what his aims are, I don't know, I suppose he wants to clarify the lectures. But I could get as much reading books.'

'When attending the seminars, now what do you aim to get out of them?'

'A page full of writing ... letters to my friends ...'.

- Obscurity as a conscious pedagogic strategy?

The only tutor who was specifically asked by a student about whether students have to understand the process he was taking them through, declared that students should be told that 'they shouldn't expect to understand it'. His response might represent more than a minority practice of what Donald Schön calls a strategy of 'mystery and mastery'.... He remarked

'... It is in the nature of that work that what is going on isn't really evident until a long time afterwards.'

Question: Do you think it's important that ... they [your students] are aware that.... Do you think they have to understand it as they do it, or ...?

Response: If you're saying, Do you want people to be able to define accurately and evaluate what they've done, then, NO, that's inappropriate for the work.... It's not that the work is mystical or incomprehensible, but you can preannounce to people that they shouldn't expect to understand it.... It would deny the experiential basis of the work to introduce it by saying that that is the type of work it is ...' (Wengraf, 1992).

DISTINGUISHING FEATURES OF THE PROJECT

On reflection, the following features seem to have been important in determining the relative success of the project.

Student 'free hand' in designing the question-schedule within a broad brief

The students were given the brief of interviewing about 'What could be done to improve the experience of a particular module?', plus the injunction to interview three people, including if possible a member of academic staff teaching on the module. The brief was deliberately unspecific to ensure that any further decisions about focus, questions and angle came from the student's own experience.

It was the first-year student who had to decide which first-year module might be worth improving, how far to identify issues in advance, and what questions to ask their student and staff informants.

The student as interviewer: confidential peer interviewing for validity

Given that students were doing the interviewing and could guarantee effective anonymity to their peers, the chances are that 'fewer punches were pulled' by peers in terms of identifying sources of dissatisfaction than might otherwise have been the case had the interviewers been staff.

The student as interviewer: problems of interviewing staff 'from below'

My impression was that those teachers who agreed to be interviewed by one of 'their' students typically were much more 'defensive' than they would have been had they been interviewed by another member of staff or by an 'outsider'. This very widespread 'defensive strategy' even on the part of staff who freely gave of their time to be interviewed suggests the difficulty that *all* staff have in having a 'free and frank exchange of views' with students about how their module or their teaching could be improved. What relations of power/knowledge (in Michel Foucault's terms) block the staff's capacity to learn how to learn from students?

Student analysing and reporting: three interviews modify the initial perspective of the student

Each student had to interview three interviewees: preferably two other students and a member of staff. All 49 students interviewed three people. Half managed to obtain an interview with a member of the teaching staff; the other half interviewed three students.

They then had to cope with the usually quite different perspectives of their three interviewees and bring them into a coherent whole. The 49 student reports in the main showed that the task of attempting to grapple with these perspectives was a source of considerable creative strain, in which the student reporter-interviewer modified his or her own perception as a result of the inquiry and reporting process. There was a clear self-educational value to the process.

Meta-analysis of full student interpretation plus sample transcript

In order to know what weight to give to the three-interview 'interpretation' section of each report, it was crucial for me as tutor to have a full transcript of [at least] one of the interviews. This made it possible to evaluate the probable strengths and weaknesses, biases and accuracy of the 'student interpretation' on the basis of a direct contact with an interview transcript. It also made it possible to use material from the transcript that the student had not used at all. Time prevented me from using the interview tapes, but these were also available for re-analysis.

Staff learning from grappling with the material from the 49 student reports

The full range of aspects selected by the interviewees and the interviewer was impressive, and the relative frequency of certain issues was informative. Similarly the variety of very different responses documented in the student reports to the same issues was also an invaluable source of insight. Given the student researcher/informant's freedom to focus on any topic, it was interesting to discover that most perplexity and dissatisfaction seemed to crystallize around the topic of 'seminars'. Students and staff typically had very contradictory views of their functions and typically never seemed to communicate effectively to each other what those views were. It is perhaps not surprising that ambiguities of power are perhaps greatest in this area.

One colleague who berated me strongly for collecting such 'unbalanced accounts' of student perceptions on the grounds that 'it would give management a stick to beat us with' (under certain conditions, this might have been and may well be a serious problem which researchers need to think about, but not under current management conditions at Middlesex) later conceded that 'the student material had made her think a lot' and she was revising her handbook for students as a result.

USES OF THE INFORMATION

Such information from students researching into student learning can then be used:

- as a basis for staff discussion and staff development training;

- as a basis for student discussion and student development training;

- as a basis for staff-student discussion in the functional equivalent of 'quality circles';

- for the development of checklists with which those in charge of modules and programmes can consider the quality of their delivery;

- for the development of institution-wide research, eg, questionnaire surveys.

WHERE CAN SUCH STUDENT RESEARCH EXERCISES AS A PART OF ORDINARY COURSEWORK LEARNING BE CARRIED OUT?

Research methodology courses

My experience suggests that 'human sciences' methodology courses can provide a suitable base in which such work can be carried out as part of the student's ordinary programme, and that semi-structured interviewing is a user-friendly point from which even first-year students can start.

The types of disciplinary programmes with such activity would include psychology, writing, humanities (eg, oral history), cultural studies, communication studies, management training, trade union studies, community studies, nursing and other service-industry vocational training where 'programme evaluation' and 'organization analysis' are relevant.

Research method strategies other than semi-structured interviewing include:

- 'focus group discussions' in themselves or (like the University of Central England in Birmingham) for the designing of a student satisfaction survey;

- the production and analysis of individual or collective 'personal autobiographical documents' as part of mini-projects in first-year methodology introductory courses, expanded versions of Records of Achievement, personal resource statements (often developed for mature students), and student logs/diaries are all suitable material for research (see for example, Ribbens, 1993).

Non-methodology courses

Substantive courses might well include similar activities: eg, in sociology, modules in the sociology of education, of work and organization, of deviance, etc. might all include such 'students as researchers into student learning' work as part of developing the substantive knowledge base of the student.

SOME FINAL QUESTIONS

Why are undergraduate students in higher education not brought to study the literature on undergraduate students in higher education?

There is a considerable knowledge base developing about student learning in mass higher education, but it is my impression that the number of undergraduate courses on which such material is systematically disseminated as an object of formal study to students is relatively small. The number of courses in which undergraduate students are enrolled as *contributing researchers* to that knowledge base is probably even fewer.

Given the importance currently being given to help students learn to learn more effectively, the failure to teach undergraduates research findings and debates about undergraduate learning and to use them as contributing researchers into student learning seems striking. No administration is spontaneously keen to empower its potential 'insider critics'. Only the most advanced 'learning organizations' take that step. Conversely, to take that step is to make a large movement towards being a very advanced 'learning organization' as described by Peter Senge (1990).

If 'action research' is defined as research in which the peer actors explore the consequences of different ways of changing the actions they engage in, then undergraduate students are only engaging completely in action research to the extent to which they (a) collectively write and discuss reports on their research, and (b) have the power to change aspects of the module design and the delivery of the curriculum and their own practice in relation to the curriculum, and explore the repercussions of such changes on their own experience.

Will not full implementation of a policy of promoting learning through student action research depend on tutors engaged in some form of power-sharing?

Despite the questions identified above, I hope that this chapter has suggested the potential value – for the students themselves, for staff, for research – of enrolling undergraduates as (action) researchers into student learning.

Acknowledgement: my thanks to Dr Chloe Stallibrass for comments on an earlier draft of this paper.

REFERENCES

Everard, K B (1993) 'Development training' in Graves, N (ed.) *Learner-Managed Learning*, Higher Education for Capability, Leeds: HEC.

Foucault, M (1989) *The Archaeology of Knowledge*, London: Routledge.

Gregory, M (1993) 'Accrediting professional development at Masters level through action research and action learning: a model for empowerment', paper presented to the Staff and Educational Development Association's conference on 'Research and Teaching in Higher Education', November, Cardiff.

Noblit, G W and Hare, R D (1988) *Meta-Ethnography: Synthesising qualitative studies*, London: Sage.

Ribbens, J (1993) 'Facts or fictions: aspects of the use of autobiographical writing in undergraduate sociology', *Sociology*, February.

Schön, D (1987) *Educating the Reflective Practitioner*, London: Jossey-Bass.

Senge, P (1990) *The Fifth Discipline: The art and practice of the learning organisation*, Uxbridge: Doubleday.

Wengraf, T (1992) *Some Reflection on Quality-Control and Customer-Satisfaction Issues Implied by First-year Student Interviews with First-year MDS Students and Staff*, Higher Education Action Research and Design Unit, Middlesex University.

Zuber-Skerritt, O (1992) *Action Research in Higher Education: Examples and reflections*, London: Kogan Page.

Chapter 18

The Relationship between Staff and Educational Development

Terri Kelly

INTRODUCTION

The growth of provision for professional development in universities is recent and rapid. New appointments, initiatives, structures and forms of professional qualifications have created a discomforting (for some) juxtaposition of 'vocational' training with 'academic' development. The weary distinctions between training and education are earnestly offered, by some, as a means of last-ditch defence as higher education becomes exposed to the 'threatening', inexorable growth of professional development opportunities. 'Training is what you do to dogs, not people', is a cherished (by the author) pronouncement by a member of teaching staff.

Given the embedded beliefs (of academic staff in higher education) about the distinctions between education and training, it might seem (to our ubiquitous Martian visitor) that the obvious providers of professional development for teaching staff are the educationists within the universities' own faculties, schools and departments of education. However, this begs the question: can the educationists who train school teachers train university teachers? Do university teachers want them to? Although there are, indeed, forms of excellent provision from the departments of education within our own walls, cynics and sceptics might argue that this discipline – education – is not always valued equally with other subject areas. Given the perceived status of the appointed providers of professional development for teaching staff, at least one challenge for these providers is to provide development opportunities in acceptable and credible ways.

The purpose of this chapter is to consider the relationship between staff development and educational development – as functions within universities. It is an intriguing phenomenon within universities that there should be a perceived bifurcation between educational development for academic staff and other forms of staff development. The first is respectable (for academics) the second is not. Even educational development activities, however, are not universally esteemed, demanded or massively subscribed to. Those of us who work within universities and who have an interest in professional development (for whatever category of staff) are confronted daily with massive ironies. We are all educationists. We are committed to the pursuit of knowledge and to enabling learning. Promoting understanding and developing reflective learners and able doers is what we are about. Universities are 'seats of learning'. Yet most of the staff who teach and research consider that their own professional development is implicit in and integral to their academic pursuits. They do not, therefore – they often feel – need any extraneous professional development.

The first section below describes an internal initiative for the University of Hull – an educational development team. The experiences to date, successes and problems, provide fascinating illustrations of received notions about 'training' in Universities. The second section explains the context for staff development at the University of Hull. The third section discusses some of the ideas surrounding educational and staff development functions.

AN EDUCATIONAL DEVELOPMENT TEAM – THE CASE STUDY

Hull University, just as every other university, has been addressing the need to support staff in achieving teaching quality. In order to provide the necessary support for effective teaching and simultaneously maintain an intended devolution of training and development, an educational development team (EDT) was established in the university during the academic session 1991/2. An internal team of (initially) six trainers/consultants, drawn from the various schools and representing the broad areas of arts, sciences and humanities was created. A senior member of academic staff (a Head of Department) undertook to be the team's coordinator. The team members have been, in effect, seconded from their departments for the equivalent of (at least) one day per week.

The initial idea for an internal team grew out of activities organized by the then dean (now EDT coordinator) and the staff development representative for the school of arts. Because of the way staff development funds and activities are organized within the University of Hull, each area has a discrete sum of money which is allocated on the basis of annual plans. Schools do not always use their funds for supporting teaching development initiatives. The school of arts did just this, though, during 1990. Then they quickly realized that bringing in external consultants for diagnosing need and designing workshops was going to consume funds very quickly and was not, perhaps, the best method for ensuring continuing skills development within the school. The school of arts proposed, therefore, in their staff development plan for 1991/2, that they develop their own school-based team of consultants.

The idea grew. The staff development officer (who had been invited to share ideas about this school initiative) suggested an ambitious extension to the school-based team project. Seeing that there was a growth of interest in enhancing teaching quality, seeing that there was (naturally enough for a higher education institution) plenty of expertise in and enthusiasm for teaching, and seeing the potential of a home-grown team, the only-begetters were persuaded to lend their efforts to establishing a university-wide 'Teaching support team' (as the project was called in its early, glimmer-in-the-eye days).

Having agreed on the merit of the university-wide team idea, the dean and the staff development officer joined forces in order to conduct an internal lobbying campaign for funds, peer support and senior management support (particularly through the adoption of appropriate institutional policies). The campaign took longer and the battle for funds and support took more persuasion than might have been anticipated! Two major, external pressures proved to be more persuasive than the earnest staff development officer and more eloquent than the exquisitely-phrased dean: the Higher Education Quality Council's three-pronged initiative, and the imminent (at that time) Higher Education Funding Council's Quality Assessment operation.

Senior managers are not that (senior) for nothing. They spotted the desirability of having palpable evidence of support for teaching which would stand up to any external scrutiny. Ironically, though, the very factors which influenced institutional support were hostages to fortune when seeking peer support. The promise of external scrutiny does not gladden the average academic's heart. Suggesting to rank-and-file teaching staff that an internal teaching support initiative will serve a political need is as sensible as linking an imposed appraisal scheme to an 'or else' pay deal. Knowing this, peer support was sought on the grounds of personal experience, personal contact and by being absolutely clear that a home-grown team would serve individuals, would not be actively serving political expediency, and would retain independence and integrity. The team would only offer training and consultancy by invitation, it would not be used to 'sort out problem staff'; whatever workshop programme it offered would be voluntarily undertaken by participants. It would not be linked to appraisal or probation.

Funding was provided in Spring 1991 (some central staff development funds were earmarked for training the team, for administrative overheads and a stock of publications and other resources. A discrete central staffing budget for seconding team members was made available on a continuing basis). Team members were recruited through an open, published invitation to apply. (Selection was augmented by word-of-mouth recommendations and by grapevine reputations.) Persuading committees to lend support had proved difficult, but persuading half-tempted potential team members that this would be a viable and rewarding project was the real challenge. 'What about my research?'; 'How will my colleagues regard me if I seem to be assuming expertise?'; 'What if they think we're management pawns?'; 'How will my depart-ment get recompense?'; 'What if they try to make us train the unre-deemable?'; 'Everyone knows that this kind of thing won't help with applications for promotion...'. The most difficult argument of all was, 'I enjoy teaching. Doing this will take time away from my work with my students – won't it?'

The first brave volunteers were slowly appeased and reassured. They did that for each other, really. Regular meetings, careful discussion and analysis and cooperation by deans and heads of department contributed to a settling-in of team-members. However, the early planning days were fraught with uncertainty. The clear good sense, good will and commit-ment of the recruited team overcame the very real knowledge that they were investing time and reputations in a high-risk initiative – and for no palpable reward. The staff development officer and the dean-become-coordinator planned ways of building the team, developing a strategic approach, agreeing objectives and designing events. It was hoped to begin a term-long programme of teaching workshops in Autumn 1991. All of Spring and Summer terms 1991 were spent in discussion, design and development. The forward plan was tenuous. The team identity was still fragile. Anxiety levels were high.

Team members suffered from a sense of unreality. They wanted (reasonably) to know what was being done in other universities and whether we would learn from similar models. The staff development officer knew of nothing quite like this Hull model but did three things: brought information about existing forms of educational development, sought external consultants who could provide ideas, reassurance and expertise and attempted to draw other universities into a collaborative extension of this home-grown team model. (This latter strategy proved abortive!) The team-members themselves drew upon their own contacts in other universities. A significant point in building the team occurred when an external ('new' university) consultant was identified.

Our consultant gave us good advice. Above all, he gave an edge of certainty and authority to the team's planning. During these develop-mental stages the team members' confidence began to build and the proposed activities took convincing shape and began to seem real. They were certainly imminent!

In October 1991 the team (now named the educational development team – EDT for brevity's sake) began a pilot workshop programme aimed primarily (but not exclusively) at staff new to teaching. The programme was well attended (but attendance eventually fell away from about 30 to an average of 15 per session) and was thoroughly reviewed and evaluated. The evaluations showed conclusively that the falling attendance was due to conflicting and growing pressures of work upon new staff. There was no great incentive for them to attend and departments simply did not always enable them to have respite from other duties.

The team had planned a number of initiatives for its first year of activity. It would:

- design and provide a workshop programme

- build a library of teaching resources

- build a bibliographical database

- undertake at least one high-profile project

- publish a newsletter

- undertake continuing development of their own teaching skills

- continue to shape medium- and long-term plans

and in order to underpin these short-term initiatives and aid long-term planning:

- aim to shape institutional policy showing clearer recognition of and reward for effective teaching.

The EDT did all of these things, though not all – the bibliographical base, for example – were completed within the year. The 'high-profile' project was a survey of 'Innovations in teaching', a beautifully produced in-house publication which revealed an impressive and heartening wealth of innovative activity. Shaping policy was successful and resulted in promotions being made on the strength of effective teaching (and being publicized as such), the use of teaching portfolios being recommended as evidence for applications for promotion, and probationers being emphatically recommended to undertake the workshop programme and build a teaching portfolio. There is more besides...
Current activities show an even healthier range of activities and policy developments:

- Funding continues (still on a continuing basis) in order to provide for staffing cover for the team members and for administrative support. It is being recognized that the EDT may now make a legitimate claim for more substantial resources.

- The number of team members has grown from six to eight full-time members (including the coordinator) and three half-time associate members.

- An additional short (but not sharp) induction programme for new staff now precedes the workshop programme and offers a 'taster' opportunity to would-be participants.

- The programme of workshops has been modified and extended and has now been validated by the University as a Higher Education Teaching Certificate. (SEDA accreditation is intended and the course has been designed to meet the required values and competences.)

- The EDT initiative has gained publicly-stated support from the vice-chancellor, who contributed to the key induction event at the start of the Autumn '93 term, and has since contributed to one of the workshops.

- Attendance on the current programme is excellent (36) and not falling away, thanks to the incentive of the Certificate, the vice-chancellor's clear support and surer, more consistent, departmental support.

- Key committees (the Board of Studies, Teaching and Learning Committee, Staff Development Committee and Academic Planning Committee) have also supported and endorsed the objectives of the initiative.

- A new Centre for Teaching and Learning has been created which includes the EDT and aims for synergy with various educational technology projects.

- The EDT is continually invited by schools and departments to help them with projects relating to teaching.

Auditors and assessors have noted and remarked upon all this! The work of our EDT; the dissemination of good practice; the growth of interest and activity in exploring teaching and learning issues; and the explicit intention within the university's promotion and advancement procedures to reward excellence in teaching have all been commended within audit and assessment reports.

THE UNIVERSITY OF HULL CONTEXT FOR STAFF DEVELOPMENT

At the commencement of the new Academic year of 1990/91, the University of Hull responded to developments within HE by rethinking and restructuring its staff development and training policy and practice. The developments which spurred this decision had emerged over the past few years. They included – at national level – major reports such as the CVCP's *Code of Practice* on *Academic Staff Training* (1987), the UCNS' *Investing in People* (1988) (now superseded by the 1993 *Promoting People* Fender Report) and the establishment of a CVCP Universities' Staff Development Unit (USDU). At regional level there were consortia planning leadership and management training, and administrative and technical staff training. At local level the university's own strategic plan to 1994/5 set out a number of aims and objectives almost all of which had clear staff development implications and requirements. Undoubtedly, these aims will be echoed in others' institutional plans and reflect the external pressures for change upon HE.

The major aspects of the restructured staff development/training policy and practice were as follows:

- The establishment of a coordinating committee chaired by a pro-vice-chancellor and representing all categories of staff.
- Inclusion of all categories of staff within the scheme.
- Appointment of a full-time officer responsible for developing and managing the scheme.
- Allocation of a sum from the central budget earmarked explicitly for staff development and training.
- Devolution of that sum, subject to submitted plans and costs, to the schools, sections and services which comprise the institution.
- In this way to give ownership, management and decision-making over to the different component parts of the university rather than to contain staff development at the centre.

It was agreed that the sum earmarked from the central budget would initially represent 1 per cent of funded salary costs, rising – subject to the university's financial position over the planning period – to at least 1.5 per cent. The sum earmarked and consequently devolved for 1990/91 was £106,000. The sum earmarked and devolved for 1991/2 was £150,000. The sums earmarked and recently devolved for 1992/3 and 1993/4 were £200,000.

There are 13 schools and 11 sections/services within the university. Once devolved, the central sum breaks down into very modest amounts. However, it is integral to the new policy that where schools, sections and services have alternative sources of revenue they contribute counterpart funds towards development and training.

A network of staff development representatives augment the potentially lonely role of the staff development officer. Recent changes have resulted in the appointment of a trainer. The 'sole operator' now has a very welcome partner who, with the two secretarial staff, make up the current staff development office team. Some of the staff development representatives for the schools, sections and services are informed and committed enthusiasts. Some are not.

RELATIONSHIPS AND ISSUES

The establishing of the EDT, described above, refers to some involvement by the university's staff development officer. Aspects of the role should, because of the purposes of this analysis, be made explicit. The staff development officer's contributions may be summarized as follows:

- identifying and expressing a university-wide need;
- persuading the active to extend ideas and activities in order to meet that need;
- using formal and informal means of communication to gain support;
- costing and wording proposals;
- researching other forms of provision;
- seeking external consultants
- helping to recruit and select team members;
- acting as internal adviser to team members;
- providing administrative back-up for all activities;
- keeping the faith!

Personal relationships between the coordinator, team members and the staff development officer are happy and relaxed and (the author maintains) based on healthy mutual respect. The team members' relationships with each other are excellent. At weekly meetings there is a lot of laughter, ideas are generated, decisions are made (most of the time) and the cut and thrust of debate is never bloody. The team has gone through the forming and norming stages. It could be said to be, currently, storming.

However, the very success of the EDT within the university is revealing some of the tensions described in the introduction to this analysis. As the EDT begins to be considered a jewel in the crown (and not such a small one, either) amorphous forces are moving, inexorably, to sever it from other staff development activities. One can now hear people referring to the absolute need for academic staff to see this as – above all – a peer-provided service. Indeed it is. It is merely that the concept of 'peer' is not universally shared.

'Do you know,' a member of staff in an Educational Development Service within another university said to the author, 'there are staff development people moving into educational development work and they know nothing about education?' The question is based upon a detectable movement in UK universities to broaden the internal base for professional development. It is also based upon the fact that in some universities, staff developers have driven the impetus to provide educational development services where only poor (or non-existent) provision existed. Because such people (whose remit is usually, but not always, for all categories of staff) drove the changes they – naturally enough – have a high profile within the new forms of provision.

A parallel movement is detectable. In some universities, especially 'new' ones, there has been excellent and well-resourced provision for educational development. This is, in places, being broadened so as to extend development and training provision to all categories of staff. 'Do you know,' a staff development adviser said to the author recently, 'there are people moving into staff development for allied staff and they know nothing about these staff or their work?'

Within the University of Hull, the establishing of a new Centre for Teaching and Learning Support is going to provide a physical space and a clearly located identity for the EDT. As plans are shaped, the continuing role of the staff development office becomes less clear. This is fine, on one level. The aim has always been to create a service which is self-sustaining. However, experience at some universities shows that where a bifurcation between educational development and 'other' staff development exists, the 'other' element becomes not-so-subtly demoted.

The word 'training' is relevant when considering these perceived attitudes and shifts of position. 'Training' is often considered to be damned by connotations of industry and commerce; demoted by comparison with that higher thing, education; dictatorial because of its directive, linear, acquisition of skills associations. The word 'training' is disappearing from letterheads, title pages and job descriptions. The

CVCP Universities' Staff Development Unit (USDU) used to be called the Universities' Staff Development and Training Unit (USDTU). The University of Hull's staff development officer used to be called the staff development and training officer. Eighteen months ago the word 'training' was dropped, 'to reflect the wider, professional development provision which is needed'. A new training officer has been appointed – at a lower grade, of course. 'I don't really believe in these "training" workshops', said a member of academic staff on his feedback form (for a management skills programme). The same member of staff *did* believe in the workshops offered by the EDT.

Some of the reasons for this mistrust of 'training' emerge from the academics' mistrust of external pressures for change in HE. 'There's something very odd about all this managerialism', wrote a veteran member of academic staff to the staff development officer upon hearing about the university's commitment to the Investors in People scheme. 'We do not simply teach; nor simply research. These two areas do not cover what we do. We are in the business of learning and teaching others how to learn. To do this professionally requires self-management.' The letter ended on a challenge: '...are you prepared to have the courage to turn your back on that other industry, management of human resources...?' Now here's a thing. No wonder academic staff – in fact, any staff – react against professional developers who refer to them as a 'resource'. The language of the professional staff developer is often guilty of reflecting a brutal, commodities-driven approach to getting the best out of people.

Political correctness and 'incorrect' political forces are undoubtedly shaping the jobs of the educational and staff development professionals. 'Write a piece for the newsletter about the political necessity for having induction programmes', invited a member of the EDT. 'Political?' asked the naive staff development officer. 'Yes, of course, political,' insisted the team-member. Some of us thought that induction programmes were a sensible, effective and humane way of bringing new staff into an organization. Perhaps not. Perhaps we must demonstrate that we are doing the right thing. The twin external scrutinies, audit and assessment, are helping to foster this cynicism. We must show that what we are doing is correct. We must appear to be doing the correct thing.

Educational development must be wrested from the hands of the 'non-educationists' – that's especially those of us who have a 'training' background. Educational development must be given over to the respectable, professional educators. An article by Professor Tim Brighouse (ex Keele) in the THES (1993) discussed the forces for change and the uncertain future for departments of education in HE. The article pointed out that:

University education departments will need to be strong and have a clear sense of purpose and identity. They will need to see their role as the acknowledged experts in teaching and learning across all the phases – from the early years to university education itself. So the education department will be the department responsible for the initial education and training both of further education lecturers in the area and of lecturers and graduate teaching assistants within its own campus. Unless it does that and leads a drive to improved quality in course design and delivery it has only a tenuous claim to exist at all within a university.

However, one of the great strengths of the University of Hull's EDT has been that it has not been created from within our school of education. We benefit extensively from having two full and one associate member drawn from the school. The school of education is a source of advice and support for the university's new teaching and learning initiatives. Colleagues, though, comment favourably upon the spread of disciplines represented within the EDT and upon the 'like us' factors which help staff to identify with and relate to the team members.

There is a growth of Masters-bearing courses provided by departments of education. These are admirable. However, most academic staff simply cannot attend over the duration required and many of these courses do not address the day-to-day context of the working academic. It is indeed true that departments of education must reposition themselves but it might be argued that their historical role has not served them well and that their colleagues in other disciplines may not easily see them as the 'acknowledged experts in teaching and learning across all the phases'.

Perhaps the home-grown team, drawing from the department of education, provides an answer to the development needs of teaching staff. Perhaps the recognition that development needs extend beyond teaching and research may improve the forms of provision for teaching staff. Finally, perhaps a recognition that professional staff and educational developers have similar expertise and complementary strengths – joining at the one word, 'learning' – may close the binary divide and hierarchical positioning of these functions.

REFERENCES

Brighouse, T (1993) 'Strong forces for change', in *THES*, 10 September.
CVCP (1987) *Code of Practice on Academic Staff Training*, Warwick: CVCP
Fender Report (1993) *Promoting People*, Warwick: CVCP.
UCNS (1988) *Investing in People*, Warwick: CVCP.

Afterword

A Manifesto for Research, Teaching and Learning

Brenda Smith and Sally Brown

Much is currently made of the dual demands placed on academics today by their sometimes conflicting responsibilities in the fields of teaching and research. We see them as being indivisible and mutually supportive: teaching which is not based on sound current research is as much of a clashing gong and a clanging cymbal as research which is held as the esoteric prerogative of the isolated ivory-tower dweller.

We conclude this book with a number of pointers we derive from our experience and that of working with the authors of the chapters in this book. The first seven points in our manifesto are concerned with a strategic approach to research, teaching and learning in higher education, with suggestions for those working at all levels within the university system on how to ensure that the students' experiences of learning are enriched by the contact they have with academic staff. The remaining three points refer to the ways in which research into teaching and learning can and must be operationalized if it is to be most effective and efficient in terms of time and money spent.

● *It is essential that the Higher Education Funding Council (HEFC) for England and Wales acknowledge the need for research into the teaching and learning processes, must fund it appropriately and must enable such research to be properly counted within subject disciplines.*
The current trend in which teachers of a specific subject, say geography, cannot have their published work on the teaching of geography counted towards their research records in the same way as their research into matters geographic can, must not be permitted to continue. At the moment it can be counted usually by the education department of the university (if such exists) rather than by the lecturer's originating department, and so by many is regarded as secondary and peripheral. If teaching quality matters (and we are assured it does) then the funding councils must put their money where their mouths are and let research about the effectiveness of teaching methods be equally valued.

● *The ways in which such research is recognized and funding apportioned must be and* must be seen to be *scrupulously fair.*

At the moment it seems to many that fairness is absent from funding decisions relating to research, both pure research and that applied to teaching. Only when the system is transparent, with the criteria and judging systems overt and open to scrutiny will we be able to be sure that justice is being done.

● *Vice-chancellors of universities need to recognize the importance of teaching and learning as the core business of higher education, must develop institutional strategies to ensure that research into its effectiveness is undertaken and must evolve appropriate and equitable reward systems for those who regard facilitation of learning as their prime function.*

Many universities are already looking at ways of rewarding excellent teachers in a way comparable to that by which excellent researchers are rewarded, and we would argue for considerable extension of this. This is not special pleading, but a demand for a strategic approach that puts in the vanguard a desire to see maintenance of and an improvement in the quality of students' learning experiences.

● *Staff and educational developers need to devise ways in which they can actively encourage research into educational practices.*

They need to provide a supportive climate in which teachers in higher education can work together to find out how effective are different methods of teaching, learning and assessment in practice. Many of us are already engaged in such activity, but we may wish to give the work a higher priority, particularly exploring the use of internal and external networks to assure more effective transfer of the benefits of individual lecturers' learning about learning to a wider context.

● *It is essential that faculties and departments set up teaching and learning groups to enable appropriate local strategies and initiatives to be designed, so that teachers feel full ownership for the pedagogical developments in which they are involved.*

Ideas on educational methods that are imposed from the top down may have some effect, but when people are talking together at the grass-roots about how best to undertake curriculum design and delivery, this will tend to have a much greater impact.

● *New lecturers need encouragement to be reflective practitioners, regularly evaluating their own teaching and learning experiences and learning from them. They should be regarding research into their own teaching and learning as an essential part of their professional lives.*

At many universities, particularly those where courses for new lecturers have achieved SEDA accreditation, lecturers are encouraged to reflect on their own practice through the use of portfolios and self-evaluative diaries, thus effectively becoming researchers into their own pedagogical practices. We would argue that these are excellent practices, not just for new lecturers but for all of us who are working with students.

● *Research students at all levels who are undertaking teaching need effective support to enable them to develop as teachers.*
Even though their individual workload may only be a few hours a week, it is important that they receive adequate support to enable them to become good teachers.In a number of universities known to the authors, first-year degree students may have up to 80 per cent of their teaching delivered by research students, who may have had minimal preparation (if any) for the task. We also know of pockets of excellence where researchers are well-prepared for the task, but these are rarer. With the advent of student charters and partnership agreements, we must ensure that all those involved in teaching are trained and supported in their work.

● *Research about teaching must be rigorous and valid.*
Appropriate methods must be chosen, including action research and all kinds of qualitative and quantitative approaches.The tendency towards anecdotal evidence must be avoided: we need convincing evidence on how well methods compare in effectiveness, particularly if we are advocating innovative practices.

● *The volume of research into teaching and learning that already exists, together with the findings of new research, must be effectively disseminated.*
Learning derived from our research must be shared by being published if we are to ensure that we make the students' experience of being taught a better one. Organizations such as SEDA, the Staff and Educational Development Association, SRHE, the Society for Research in Higher Education, the Open Learning Foundation and the Universities' Staff Development Unit must all continue to be involved in effective dissemination of research findings through conferences and publications (see Chapter 2). With Graham Gibbs, we would welcome the setting up of a national centre for research into teaching and learning in higher education with overall responsibility for this function.

● *Staff and educational developers must ourselves be reflective in our practice too.*
We must use all means available to research how effective we are being, not just in achieving our specified objectives, but also in affecting the cultures of our own universities and the higher education system as a whole. We need to know how great is the impact of our own work in bringing about productive change, so we can channel our energies accordingly and feed into the quality loop.

THE CASE FOR A HOLISTIC APPROACH

Each of the ten points we propose, if implemented successfully, could contribute significantly towards improving the quality of experience for both students and lecturers in higher education. Taken together, however, they provide a holistic strategy which could radically change for the better the ways in which universities work, ensuring that the relationship between research and teaching is symbiotic rather than conflictual and producing an environment in which *learning* is central to the practice of all.

Index